san francisco ballet
at seventy-five

WITHDRAWN

san francisco ballet
at seventy-five

By Janice Ross

Preface by Brigitte Lefèvre   Foreword by Allan Ulrich

Text copyright © 2007 by Janice Ross.
Preface copyright © 2007 by Brigitte Lefèvre.
Foreword copyright © 2007 by Allan Ulrich.
Photographs copyright © by individual photographers.
Page 187 constitutes a continuation of the copyright page.

All rights reserved.
No part of this book may be reproduced in any form
without written permission from the publisher.

Library of Congress Cataloguing-in-Publication Data available.

ISBN-10: 0-8118-5698-4
ISBN-13: 978-0-8118-5698-0

Manufactured in China.

Distributed in Canada by Raincoast Books
9050 Shaughnessy Street
Vancouver, British Columbia V6P 6E5

10 9 8 7 6 5 4 3 2 1

Chronicle Books LLC
680 Second Street
San Francisco, California 94107

www.chroniclebooks.com

2–3) Helgi Tomasson's
Swan Lake (2006)

4–5) Ruben Martin in
Stanton Welch's *Tu Tu*
(2003)

6–7) Kristin Long (left)
and Lorena Feijoo (right)
in Yuri Possokhov's
Reflections (2005)

8–9) Jaime Zimmerman,
Christopher Boatwright,
Evelyn Cisneros, and
Lawrence Pech in James
Kudelka's *Dreams of
Harmony* (1987)

San Francisco Ballet and
the San Francisco Ballet School
gratefully acknowledge the
leadership and support of several
of their longtime supporters and
special sponsors of the Seventy-Fifth
Anniversary celebrations.

Major Sponsors

Richard and Rhoda Goldman Fund

Yurie and Carl Pascarella

Sponsors

Stuart Francis and Diana Stark

Stephen and Margaret Gill
Family Foundation

Chris and Warren Hellman

Cecilia and Jim Herbert

George Frederick Jewett Foundation,
Lucille Jewett, Trustee

Barbara Ravizza and John Osterweis

Kathleen Scutchfield

The Smelick Family

The Swanson Foundation

Ms. Susan A. Van Wagner

E.L. Wiegand Foundation, Reno, Nevada

Diane B. Wilsey

Akiko Yamazaki and Jerry Yang

Sponsors

Contents

PREFACE

Brigitte Lefèvre

Each time San Francisco Ballet performs in France, we recognize that we are in the presence of a vibrant and artistic dance community. In 2001, our government's Ministry of Culture and Communications granted the rank of Officer in the Order of Arts and Letters to the company's artistic director, Helgi Tomasson. The award is an important declaration for the people of France and an honor not lightly bestowed. It means that Helgi is an eminent artistic personality in the international world of arts and culture.

Great arts institutions and their leaders derive from their unique position in culture and history. Since Helgi took the helm of the United States' oldest professional ballet company, dance has undergone an intense period of change both abroad and in the United States. Following the deaths of George Balanchine and Jerome Robbins—two of the most important American choreographers working in the twentieth century—many wondered about the direction of ballet. Under Helgi's leadership, San Francisco Ballet has emerged as one of the most innovative and respected ballet companies in the world.

The company's reputation undoubtedly lies in the dancers Helgi has assembled and the repertory San Francisco Ballet now commands. Capturing the essence of classical ballet and revealing the relevance of dance in a modern world are goals that Helgi has sought and accomplished. In the process, he has also revitalized ballet audiences in the United States and, I might add, around the world.

Helgi is keenly aware that excellence in directing a great arts institution stems from creativity. In addition to his many responsibilities as an artistic director, he is also a gifted choreographer. He has invited some of his generation's most notable choreographers to create new ballets on this company, demonstrating an inspiring commitment to new work. Under his tenure, guest artists and dancers relish the opportunity to work with San Francisco Ballet because it is a place where tradition, creative expression, and artistic excellence are valued, respected, and celebrated.

As an artistic director, Helgi has created a very particular way of leading a company. He is reflective and respectful of others, and he knows where he wants to go and where he wants to lead San Francisco Ballet. He can give the impression that he is both reserved and passionate. Perhaps because he is Icelandic, he possesses a certain "fire and ice" quality that makes him unique. In the end, there is only the desire to serve a company that he sincerely loves and believes in.

On behalf of Paris Opera Ballet, I am honored to wish San Francisco Ballet and its artists and dancers a very happy seventy-fifth anniversary. As always, we look forward to seeing the company rise to new heights.

10–11) Mark Morris's *Sylvia* (2006)

12–13) Yuri Possokhov (left) and Damian Smith (right) in Christopher Wheeldon's *Quaternary* © (2006)

FOREWORD

Allan Ulrich

On the eve of San Francisco Ballet's seventy-fifth anniversary, the temptation to play the nostalgia card is irresistible.

How easily one recalls the details of so many enchanted evenings with the company. Just a few among the unforgettable moments—Evelyn Cisneros's sublime balances amid the golden onion domes in the company's first *Sleeping Beauty;* the dunce caps, dizzying extensions, and pounding score of William Forsythe's *New Sleep;* the tidal wave of affection sweeping through the audience after Joanna Berman's farewell *Giselle;* the lethal majesty of Lucia Lacarra's Novice in Jerome Robbins's *The Cage;* the visceral effect of dozens of spinning bodies at the end of the company's first performance of George Balanchine's *Symphony in Three Movements.*

I could go on, but my point has been made. We are told that the rosy glow of memory is an illusion. We're assured that the last folks to spot a golden age are those who are living through it. I disagree with that assertion.

I have been disagreeing with it three or four evenings a week, four months a year, for the past two decades. Anybody who has followed San Francisco Ballet's ascent in the local, national, and international artistic communities has come to cherish the special grace of the company. Something of uncommon significance has been happening here since Helgi Tomasson became artistic director of San Francisco Ballet in 1985, and his accomplishment heralds a major shift in thinking about the direction and future of classical dance in this country. During his tenure, Tomasson has propelled the company to the highest level in the Bay Area, where his troupe now shares the laurels equally with the San Francisco Symphony and San Francisco Opera.

On the American scene, Tomasson has created a new category of ballet company. There really is no word for it. Because the organization is located a continent away from New York, San Francisco Ballet will unjustly be denied a "national" company honorific. Yet, only the most benighted soul would call San Francisco Ballet a "regional" company. There is nothing remotely regional about an institution that employs more than seventy dancers, gives more than one hundred performances a year, operates on a $37 million budget, owns its home, and boasts an unbroken, fifteen-year record of generating surpluses.

The company's influence, however, has been truly global. The international roster of dancers who irradiate our evenings and the list of eminent choreographers whose dances dazzle our eyes testify to the excitement sparked around the world by San Francisco Ballet's appearances. This is no idle claim for those like myself who have witnessed the company's reception in Tokyo, Singapore, New York, Copenhagen, and Paris.

There is no dream without a dreamer. Whose dream was San Francisco Ballet? It is Tomasson's, his dancers' and artistic staff's, the board of trustees', and the audience's. But I can't help recalling the prophecy uttered more than two decades ago by the company's president, Richard LeBlond Jr. It was he who proclaimed that the map was tipping, that the center of American dance was rolling from east to west, and that San Francisco Ballet, the oldest professional company in this country, would be the logical place for the tradition to advance to the next plateau.

Since then, Tomasson has incorporated and commissioned a more diverse repertory than any other American ballet company in this generation. He has enforced a level of performance in which dancers have implemented their technical accomplishment with a profound understanding of why they are moving through space.

All this has happened in an era when classical dance has been under attack from within the profession, and without. Ballet, some of its critics claim, is dated, dehumanizing to dancers, and culturally irrelevant. Yet, the vast variety of approaches to classicism introduced by Tomasson and the expressive warmth that permeates the company's performances at every level refute those charges whenever the curtain rises.

Wonders like San Francisco Ballet do not happen without the synchrony, trust, and mutual respect that must exist in any performing arts organization of stature. Janice Ross's text will fill you in on the complex relationships that bind the artistic and administrative wings and the governing board of the company in a common purpose.

Ultimately, though, San Francisco Ballet in this seventy-fifth year has been informed by Tomasson's artistic and personal values. I have never met a more dedicated, more decent, or more discreet figure in the performing arts. Even in private conversation, you will not hear from his mouth a disparaging word about any of his colleagues (though you might catch a perceptive phrase or two). These twenty-two years, I believe, have been as much a voyage of exploration for Tomasson as they have for us in the audience. He has probably surprised himself more than once.

Among the many strategies Tomasson learned from George Balanchine were the arts of challenging dancers and astonishing audiences. They surfaced very early here, when Tomasson programmed Mr. B's terribly demanding *Theme and Variations*. We were dubious about the company's ability to dance a work of such legendary difficulty; we were rebuked brilliantly. Since then, Tomasson has continually raised the bar (and the barre). Who, two decades ago, could have predicted that San Francisco Ballet would cover itself in glory in a romantic classic like *Giselle* or in such fragile contemporary masterpieces as Balanchine's *Liebeslieder Walzer*, Jerome Robbins's *Dances at a Gathering,* and Frederick Ashton's *Symphonic Variations*?

Tomasson's San Francisco Ballet thrives on surprises that reflect on the company's elevated position on the international dance scene. The 1995 UNited We Dance festival gathered thirteen companies from five continents on the War Memorial stage. The highlight of the seventy-fifth anniversary season—the unveiling within a single week of ten commissioned dances by major choreographers, most of whom shaped San Francisco Ballet's unique profile during the first two decades of Tomasson's stewardship—epitomizes programming flair and daring. Has any other American ballet company ever undertaken a project of this magnitude?

One of the grayest of gray eminences in my profession once cautioned me that critics should never feel gratitude for artistic accomplishment; we should demand the best. Events of the past twenty-two years have forced me to disregard that maxim.

I will remain forever grateful to Helgi Tomasson. No other dance company has made me look harder and longer. No other company has made me feel quite so privileged to be in its presence on a regular basis. No other company has focused my thoughts so intensely about classical dance, its evolution, and its future.

It is not too early to speak of a dynasty. Back in the 1970s and 1980s, retired members of New York City Ballet, like Tomasson, founded and assumed the artistic direction of companies across the map from Seattle to Miami. Flash forward two decades. You will now find Tomasson's former dancers running the shows in Cincinnati, Boston, and Portland. The degree to which they extend and enrich the twenty-first century tradition of ballet in America may prove San Francisco Ballet's and Tomasson's most enduring legacy.

INTRODUCTION

The more perfected a body's image in the public sphere, the more hidden its preparation. Professional dancers' bodies are among the most supremely refined human forms in the world and the most secreted as they are being formed. A ballet dancer's career consists of ninety-five percent preparation compared with the five percent when she is actually onstage before a live audience.

I have spent three decades looking at dance professionally from a distance designed to keep this divide constant. I have honored the privacy of the hidden and analyzed the significance of the exposed, first as a contributing editor to *Dance Magazine* and then as staff dance critic for the *Oakland Tribune*, when it was a metropolitan daily. Subsequently, as a dance historian and academic, I have watched and written about dance, and always my interest has been in preserving and honoring this separation.

When I was asked to write this portrait of San Francisco Ballet on the eve of its seventy-fifth year, my charge was to create a comprehensive picture of the company in the present, informed by its rich historical past. I was given permission to look where I wanted and when I wanted. This brought with it the enviable dilemma: Where *do* you look if suddenly you are allowed to see it all? Company class, studio rehearsals, guest choreographers at work, orchestra rehearsals, the backstage crew changing sets, costume fittings, dressers and makeup artists at work, board of trustee meetings, donor events—it was a dance writer's shopping spree.

Like a cultural tourist, I found myself perusing the company's rehearsal schedule daily as it was posted and devising impossibly ambitious itineraries where I would bounce between watching a Balanchine expert rehearse the principals in *Apollo* in one studio and Helgi Tomasson refine his yet-to-be-premiered *Blue Rose* in another, then peek in to see former Paul Taylor star Patrick Corbin brushing up Taylor's *Spring Rounds* in yet another. A typical midweek schedule in early February began with a choice between sitting in on Tomasson teaching the men in a divided company class in the morning while Ashley Wheater taught the women in an adjacent studio. Fifteen minutes after class ended, rehearsals started and continued with three or four different rehearsals scheduled each hour, filling all four of the studios on the fourth floor in the ballet building and often the dance studio in the Opera House as well. This level of activity extended nonstop until a dinner break, after which the dancers returned and signed in at 7:30 p.m. at the ballet office inside the Opera House stage door for an 8 p.m. performance of *Swan Lake*. Then my dilemma became where to be during the performance. Backstage or in the audience? In the hallway with the dresser outside the principal women's dressing rooms, or in the brass section of the orchestra pit with the musicians, who can see only the top corner of the stage?

Altogether, the experience was humbling, exciting, and addictively pleasurable. There was beauty and transformation at every turn, and the exhilaration of being in the midst of a group of phenomenally talented, incredibly hard-working young artists under intense pressure to produce art of the highest quality and to the most exacting standards.

In doing the research for *San Francisco Ballet at Seventy-Five,* I found myself shuttling perceptually between the normally very separate worlds of the concealed and the revealed. At times within the space of the few minutes it took to walk from the stage manager's control panel backstage in the Opera House to a seat with the audience in the orchestra, I transitioned from the vantage point of insider to outsider. The backstage world of professional ballet is immensely seductive because it is all about process. One constantly sees the work, as well as some of the play, that undergirds each moment of art. Yet, paradoxically, the one thing that is impossible to see from behind the scenes is the full dance—that can be viewed in its entirety only from the audience side of the theater.

In this book, I have tried to represent these multiple views, and the fascination of the partial ones, balancing a journalistic reporting style in describing what goes on behind the scenes with a more scholarly historical analysis in order to position San Francisco Ballet critically in the larger world of contemporary culture. It is some sense of this I hope to convey in this portrait of the company, and by extension American ballet in a period of significant ascendance.

I have been writing about San Francisco Ballet since 1974, so my viewing history with the company parallels the last thirty years of its growth and its full development under Helgi Tomasson. I first interviewed Tomasson on February 4, 1985, the same week in which he retired as a dancer with New York City Ballet and, as San Francisco Ballet's new artistic director to be, flew to San Francisco to watch the company for the first time in the Opera House. "It's been quite an eventful week," he told me then with his trademark understatement about the most dramatically transitional seven days in his professional life.

As I write this almost exactly twenty-one years from the late summer date when Tomasson began as artistic director, that eventful week has led into his nearly quarter-century tenure at the helm of San Francisco Ballet. His leadership in turn has capped with brilliance what has been a more than eventful seventy-five years for America's oldest professional ballet company.

14–15) Yuri Possokhov's
Study in Motion (2005)

15

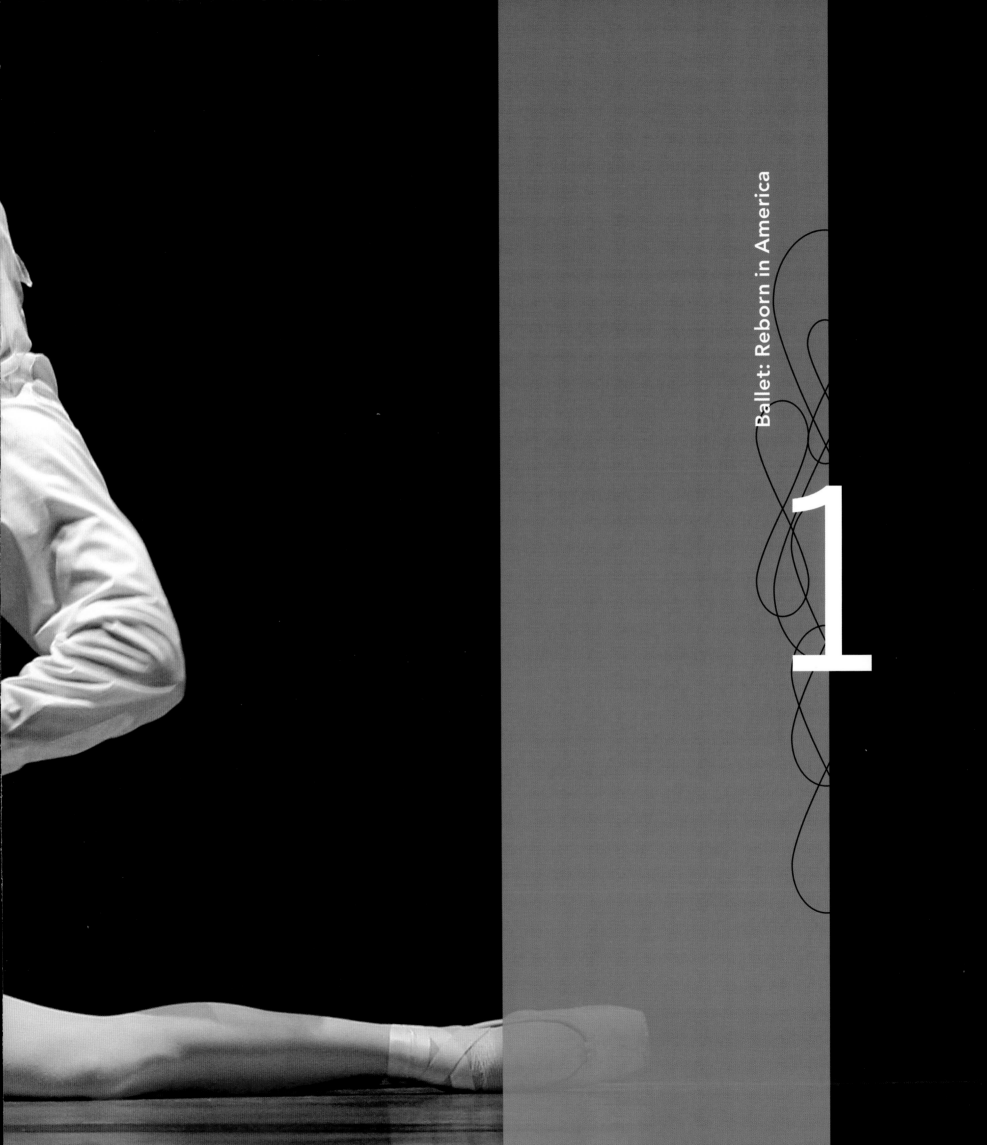

1

Birth and Renewal

San Francisco Ballet was born June 2, 1933. It was reborn August 1, 1985, when Helgi Tomasson became the company's fourth artistic director. In its first half century under the leadership of three Christensen brothers, Willam, Harold, and Lew, San Francisco Ballet led the pioneering era of ballet in the United States. In the next quarter century, Tomasson advanced and globalized San Francisco Ballet and, with it, American dance.

The story of how San Francisco Ballet began, and how it has grown and thrives, is a narrative with threads that extend deep into the lives of individuals, their cities, and the art form. Each thread reveals something about the complex role of ballet and superbly primed dancers' bodies in civic life and the public imagination. Dance artists are driven by an alchemy of necessity and vision, and dance audiences and benefactors by the pleasures of associating with that vision and making possible its realization.

16–17) Yuan Yuan Tan and Damian Smith in Yuri Possokhov's *Magrittomania* (2006)

18) Willam Christensen (center) and company dancers (left to right) Lois Treadwell, Celena Cummings, Jocelyn Vollmar, Peter Nelson, and Onna White in front of San Francisco Ballet's first studio on Van Ness Avenue (1945)

19) Helgi Tomasson choreographs in the studio (1986)

20–21) Helgi Tomasson
leads company class
(2005)

22) The War Memorial
Opera House

Toward a Global Identity

In 1933 no one knew if a resident ballet company could survive in the United States, particularly in the far west in San Francisco—if the dancers, choreographers, audiences, and patrons to sustain it could be found. Seventy-five years later, having withstood dramatic changes of direction, finances, and personnel, San Francisco Ballet has reinvented itself along with important aspects of the art of classical ballet. As it moves toward the century mark, the company is among the most international in the world, with artists from more than twenty nations represented among its dancers, staff, and choreographers. It reflects the shift away from assimilation—the old social norm in the United States at the start of the last century—and toward identity articulation, where differences are celebrated and highlighted. The diverse styling of the foreign-born dancers in the company is honored today as a key part of the growing international profile of American ballet.

Pascal Molat, a principal dancer, who trained at the Paris Opéra School and performed with several European companies before joining the company in 2003, says, "The internationality of this company is its strongest point. When Helgi hires you, he hires you for what you are. Because I am French, maybe I will think a bit differently or have another point of view from somebody who is Japanese or who is American or Russian. He likes that all of the ideas we have about dancing can fuse into one. It doesn't mean that I'm going to lose my French flair, because it's not about a style—it's more about your personality." Spanish-born principal dancer Gonzalo Garcia, who trained in Zaragoza, Spain, before coming to the San Francisco Ballet School and moving up through the ranks to become a principal dancer in 2002, agrees. He notes that the company's diverse nationalities play out with particular excitement in the studio. "It's like a dictionary of styles. You see the same step done by French, Cuban, Russian, and Australian dancers and everybody does it beautifully and you see what maybe you could use. Allowing personalities to float without crashing the whole picture. This is very rare."

American-born principal dancer Christopher Stowell, who joined the company in 1985, the first year of Tomasson's tenure, and left in 2002 to direct the Oregon Ballet Theatre, recalls the collateral learning environment this international mix inspired. "It was clear what Helgi thought each of our greatest strengths was. I remember watching Gennadi Nedvigin for *The Sleeping Beauty* stylistic issues and he'd watch me for technical things about Balanchine's choreography."

The Beginnings

The first visionary of San Francisco Ballet was a Naples-born conductor, Gaetano Merola, San Francisco Opera's general director. In 1933 Merola decided that he needed a resident opera ballet company to properly display his grand new opera house and San Francisco Opera's growing professionalism. Eleven years earlier, the popular and charismatic Merola had convinced a group of San Francisco's music-loving philanthropists that the city could support its own opera company. He was determined to create that company on a world scale.

The new opera house, which opened in October 1932, had been an important step. The breadth of San Francisco's support for its opera house, the only municipally owned opera house in the United States, was unprecedented. In addition to the usual few wealthy patrons, hundreds of working-class people had contributed small sums as founding members. With this broad base and a new grand stage for dancing came a mandate for musically and theatrically captivating ballet performances. San Francisco has never had the large number of extremely wealthy arts patrons of eastern cities. Instead, the cultural passion of a broader public and, later, the support of private local foundations and corporations have been essential to San Francisco Ballet's success and, indirectly, to the development of the company's aesthetic.

The ballet's majestic home theater, the War Memorial Opera House, was outfitted like a grandly inspirational public library with an elegant coffered ceiling in the main foyer lighted by huge bronze standing lamps. On each side of the foyer hung antique French tapestries, and double marble stairways with brass balustrades ascended to upper floors. The building of the Opera House in the midst of the Great Depression was regarded by some San Franciscans as entertainment itself, and many watched the eighteen months of construction with fascination. The Opera House continues to have a strong presence in San Francisco Ballet's life. Dennis Hudson, the genial master electrician for the company since 1971, oversees the four stories of backstage facilities with deep affection for the superb functionality of the building, now in its eighth decade. From the vintage nineteenth-century thunder and lightning machines tucked high in the attic to the two-story drop well where backdrops can be hung without bending—a remnant from the days of brittle hand-painted scenery—to the wall of weighted rigging ropes that a crew pulls to fly curtains and set pieces noiselessly on and off the stage, the Opera House is both historic and supremely functional.

The Opera House was conceived as part of the monumental civic complex of Beaux Arts buildings forming the political, judicial, and cultural center of San Francisco. While the rest of the nation struggled through the Depression, the city's economy was buffered by other big construction projects during the same period, including the groundbreaking for the Golden Gate Bridge and the Bay Bridge and the completion of Coit Tower.

Merola, who had directed San Francisco Opera since 1923, had a good eye for dance. Ballet had been part of his earliest opera productions. With the move into the new Opera House, Merola wanted to expand the ballet company and stabilize and strengthen it. He had already endured five different ballet masters during his first ten seasons. Merola is quoted in 1933 as "pleading that an opera without a school for chorus and ballet lacked one of the essentials of success." To make his point he threatened to cancel Nicolai Rimsky-Korsakov's *Le Coq d'Or* in the coming season rather than stage it without a skilled ballet master to drill the ensemble.

23

Even before he formally established the opera ballet, Merola had already sought out a reputed professional Russian dancer, Serge Oukrainsky, as ballet master in San Francisco for the 1928–30 seasons. Oukrainsky, who was of Hungarian descent, had been a soloist with Anna Pavlova, and he and fellow dancer Andreas Pavley had both been principal dancers and ballet masters for the Chicago Grand Opera Company from 1917 to 1922. Oukrainsky also directed their independent company, the Pavley-Oukrainsky Ballet, in Chicago for nine years. Oukrainsky's style, a flashy hybrid of the romanticized Orientalist repertory of Pavlova and the theatricalized dance rituals of the American modern dance troupe Denishawn, was particularly well suited to Hollywood. He alternated his time in San Francisco and Chicago with work choreographing for feature films.

The early worlds of opera and ballet in the United States were small and closely connected. For a time the Pavley-Oukrainsky Ballet was the oldest American ballet company, having been founded in 1922. But when it disbanded in 1931, after the thirty-nine-year-old Pavley died in a mysterious fall, it lost that claim. San Francisco Ballet would step into the title of the oldest professional ballet company in America in 1933. Ballet companies were also being established in England. Ninette de Valois, a British former dancer with Serge Diaghilev's Ballets Russes, founded the Academy of Choreographic Art in London in 1929, the precursor to the Royal Ballet, which started officially in May 1931. De Valois absorbed several former Ballets Russes dancers into her company after Diaghilev died suddenly in 1929, resulting in a huge exodus of Russian dancers and choreographers from Eastern Europe to the West. England and the United States were among the first beneficiaries. The transplanting of classical ballet had begun.

24) Julia Adam and Yuri Possokhov in Stanton Welch's *Maninyas* (1998)

The dapper Oukrainsky, who was sometimes described as aloof and snobbish about his pedigreed dance background and well-proportioned body, left the Chicago Grand Opera Company in 1922 when he was replaced by a bigger Russian star. That star was the celebrated Diaghilev dancer Adolph Bolm. Ruggedly handsome and athletic, Bolm was known for the gusto and ferocity of his character dancing and later his modernist choreography. When Merola hired him in 1933 as the first director of the San Francisco Opera Ballet, Bolm brought his popularity in the world of dance and his boundless energy to San Francisco. It was Bolm who founded and directed the San Francisco Opera Ballet School in addition to serving as ballet master, teaching and rehearsing the dancers. Although the opera ballet's primary purpose was to train dancers for the operas, it was, from inception, also permitted to present independent dance programs. On June 2, 1933, a capacity crowd turned out to see the first of these at the Opera House. This inaugural "all-dance" program, as it was called, was also "all-Bolm," since he choreographed the eleven dances on the program, staged and costumed the majority of them, and danced in four of the ballets.

The biggest hit of the evening was Bolm's experimentalist factory fantasy, *Le Ballet Mécanique*, which he choreographed to a pounding score by Alexander Mossolov for a cast of fifty dancers who moved with mechanistic precision like parts of a huge machine. The opera ballet was not shy about the scale of its achievement. The program notes announced, "By this premiere performance San Francisco definitely takes its place as a ballet producing center . . . the only city in the country other than New York with its Metropolitan to boast an operatic chorus and ballet school as an auxiliary to an established grand opera company." The notion of ballet as a homegrown art was taking root across the nation. For the first time it was becoming possible for Americans to get decent ballet training in the United States. Dances such as *Le Ballet Mécanique* suggested how pliable the form might be for modern subjects like the assembly line of the Ford Motor Company factory, one of the images that served as Bolm's inspiration. Initially the model for ballet had been Russian and European, and the centers had been the old opera ballets in Paris, Italy, and Russia, but now each adaptation was giving it more of an American flavor.

The new San Francisco Opera Ballet was proud of its association with the opera, but with it came expectations that would soon strain these ties. Standing-room-only crowds attended the opera ballet's second gala dance evening a year later on June 8, 1934. Bolm, tireless, offered thirteen ballets this time, designing the lighting as well as most of the costumes, and doing the staging and featured dancing. San Francisco was emerging as an established cultural destination—it was a cosmopolitan city with progressive politics, enthusiastic and increasingly knowledgeable audiences, a well-supported symphony and opera, and now one of the grandest theaters and biggest stages for dance in the nation. For the next seven decades, the Opera House stage would attract dancers and choreographers from around the world eager to dance on it and see their choreography performed on it.

Film fragments from those first years of the opera ballet show remarkably crisp ensemble dancing with a full orchestra and before an audience giving tumultuous applause to each mastery of difficult footwork and speeding turns. The dancing is serious and demanding.

After several acclaimed seasons of opera ballets and summer tours to Los Angeles with programs devoted to ballet, Bolm's contract was not renewed for the 1937 season. According to some reports, this was because Bolm complained that fall operas did not include enough ballet. Months of speculation about his possible successor followed.

The two most famous Russian choreographers in the United States, George Balanchine and Michel Fokine, were mentioned as possibilities. Leo Staats, *maître de ballet* at the Paris Opéra, was also suggested as a replacement. But the San Francisco Opera's management, which was almost all Italian, quickly rejected the notion of hiring a Frenchman. Nationalist allegiances ran deep, as did assumptions about artistic talent and its ties to certain ethnicities. At the last minute Oukrainsky was brought in again, just for the fall season, while Merola continued canvassing for a permanent ballet master and choreographer.

The Christensen Legacy Begins

In the four years since San Francisco Opera Ballet had begun, it acquired a reputation in the national press as "one of the strongest outposts of the Russian tradition in ballet in the United States." An *American* tradition in ballet had also been quietly building during the same period and would emerge over the next several years as an American voice in ballet. This sensibility would be manifested in the speed, attack, precision, and expansiveness of the dancers' use of the four-hundred-year-old ballet vocabulary, the physical challenges of the ballets they performed, and eventually the democratic mix of body types, training histories, and national identities they represented.

The San Francisco Opera Ballet would add a new first to its list—and this one was substantive. It would soon become the first opera ballet headed by dancers born and trained in the United States—dancers whose dancing lives unfolded *here* rather than abroad, as had been the case for the first generation of American modern dancers like Isadora Duncan and Loie Fuller. With the beginning of the tenure of Icelandic-born Helgi Tomasson at San Francisco Ballet in 1985—a protégé of George Balanchine, the most gifted foreign choreographer working in the United States—ballet in this country started to reflect the opening of long-closed national borders as dancers from nations as disparate as Estonia, Armenia, Russia, and China found their way to Tomasson and the company.

Ballet was ready for a fresh image, an Americanized one instead of the Euro-Russian image from French, Italian, and Russian schools of training that had predominated for decades and, in some instances, centuries. Since his arrival in New York in 1933, Balanchine had been creating a hybrid ballet style beginning with his founding of the School of American Ballet, a center to create dancers. In his first ballet in the United States, the splendidly plotless *Serenade* in 1934, Balanchine fused the complex choreographic structures of Marius Petipa, the French choreographer working in Russia, and his associate, the Russian Lev Ivanov, with a new expansiveness and propulsive drive. Abstraction and risk were becoming part of this new ballet style that dispensed with traditional storytelling in favor of celebrating the logic of musically responsive and athletically charged dancers.

Balanchine was building these ballets-without-plots on the bodies of American dancers. Among the first was Lew Christensen, who would subsequently use this training as a basis for what he developed in San Francisco. Christensen, a youth from rural Utah, would become the first great American male ballet dancer and, by the 1950s, the man central to building San Francisco Ballet's reputation. Balanchine said of Christensen that no male performer outside Russia could match him as a premier dancer in the classical style, a *danseur noble*. This legitimization by Balanchine—the man whose choreography, and the training necessary to perform it, effectively began the American style in neoclassical ballet—signaled that the United States could have a ballet tradition and that Christensen would help draft it.

As Balanchine was moving toward an American-inflected vocabulary in ballet, brothers Willam, Harold, and Lew Christensen were discovering themselves as teachers and dancers. Initially their path to the stage was routed through popular culture—twice-daily vaudeville shows where they performed a flashy ballet number sandwiched between variety acts. This was the only place outside opera or backing up a touring foreign star dancer where native ballet dancers, particularly males, could get experience creating, staging, and performing on the road in the United States in the 1920s.

This balance of familiarity with both the classical and the vernacular has defined the performing background of every director and co-director of San Francisco Ballet, from Willam and Lew Christensen and Lew's co-director Michael Smuin to Helgi Tomasson. As a teenage ballet student, Tomasson spent summers dancing in the tiny Pantomime Theatre in Copenhagen's Tivoli Gardens, miming commedia dell'arte characters in productions dating back centuries.

The Christensen brothers' grandfather, Lars, had converted to Mormonism and emigrated from Denmark to Utah in the early 1850s, bringing with him a love of music and dance. Making music and social dancing were encouraged in the Christensen children from an early age. Playing an instrument, teaching dance, and performing in vaudeville were seen as skills that could be turned into a career. One of Lars's sons, Moses, discovered ballet and began training under the Italian master Stefano Mascagno. By the early 1920s three of Moses's nephews were recruited to study classical ballet as well. There is scant mention of the Christensen girls learning dance, reinforcing this art training as a tacit rehearsal of respectable life skills for a wage earner.

For several years the Christensen trio studied, taught, and participated in recitals at Uncle Pete Christensen's family Le Crist School of Dancing in Ogden, Utah, which Willam had renamed in 1926 to add a European aura. Willam, at twenty-seven the oldest of the trio of young dancing Christensens, was restless to perform for bigger audiences. Recruiting Lew and two young female dancers from the school and borrowing its name, he created a musical dance act, Le Crist Revue. Early in the summer of 1927, Le Crist Revue arrived in Los Angeles and by August had its first real engagement at the Los Angeles Hippodrome. Billed not as ballet but "European Dance Novelty," the group was invited to tour as the second act on the Berkoff's Russian Music and Dance Show. Wearing shiny satin Cossack pants and shirts, they became the Berkoffs and went on the road. For the next seven years they toured the United States and Canada, substituting Harold for Willam when he left to direct the new branch of the family ballet school in Portland, Oregon.

FINANCING VISION

Ballet's grand achievement in the United States has always gone hand in hand with grand benefactors. Chris and Warren Hellman have been a uniquely steady team of wisdom and support on the San Francisco Ballet board of trustees, beginning in 1983 when Warren deferred an invitation to join the board to his wife. "She's the dancer," he told them. Warren, a respected investment banker, and Chris, a former soloist with London Festival Ballet, both ended up actively serving the board, Chris directly, leading with candor and artistry for sixteen years, eight of those as chair, and Warren indirectly, as a source of business and financial expertise.

"When I came on board the ballet was in the red," Chris recalls. "So I asked Warren if he would mind looking at the numbers." Where she saw danger with the company's $3 million deficit and annual losses of $1 to $1.5 million, Warren saw the familiar ups and downs of a business. "Bureaucracies don't change unless there is a crisis," he says with the Talmudic wisdom he favors. "In times of crisis, all things become possible."

While Chris tightened up the board, removing the distractions by slamming her shoe on the table at the first meeting she attended in order to stop the social chatter, Warren tidied up the ballet's financial image, writing a personal check to cover the ballet's $1 million deficit in 1990 and regaining its good standing so individual and institutional support resumed. Chris was frank with Helgi Tomasson about what the budget could and could not support—in 1991 a new ballet or touring, but not both. "Helgi understood completely. He's a very intelligent man," Chris says. Touring won, and as the ballet's reputation grew so did its audiences, donors, possibilities, and new fiscal intelligence.

In the mid-1990s, Warren was drafted to co-chair the Preserving a San Francisco Jewel stabilization campaign with John Osterweis and Bob Muh. Raising $33 million, it had a two-pronged impact of building up the endowment and providing much-needed operating cash. Along the way he founded the first West Coast–based Web site for informed discussion, critical analysis, and debate about dance, Voice of Dance. The social side of philanthropy interests the Hellmans much less than the activist role. "I'm not interested in parties and gowns," Chris says. "I tend not to go to those things. I'd much rather watch rehearsals or company class—the everyday stuff nobody cares about." Warren, who jogs every morning at 4 A.M., jokes that he never knew ballets had second acts—he's always home asleep after the first intermission.

Lucy Jewett, a generous trustee since 1969 and a passionate devotee of the dancers, shares the Hellmans' dislike of the limelight. "We're not really public people," she says of herself and husband Fritz. "The only reason we support the ballet is to make sure the company can be sane." From the board perspective, one of the biggest markers of that sanity is that the company has been in the black for fifteen years. "Helgi has seldom gone over budget," Jewett says, noting implicitly that the company's longest-running dance is the pas de deux it performs annually between the trustees' recommendations and the budget's constraints.

To build a strong financial foundation for San Francisco Ballet, the board of trustees launched the Performing at the Pinnacle Campaign in 2005. This $35 million endowment campaign will provide funds to help realize the Ballet's artistic and institutional priorities beyond the 75th Anniversary. It will solidify San Francisco Ballet's place as leader in the dance world.

27) (left to right)
Marlene Tomasson,
Artistic Director
Helgi Tomasson,
and Chris Hellman,
board of trustees chair,
1992–99

28) George Balanchine's
Apollo (2006)

America's dancing dynasty, as the Christensens would later be dubbed, was assembling the pieces of a new dance theater legacy. The act came increasingly to highlight Lew's technical virtuosity and skills as a partner. New York City Ballet's great patron, Lincoln Kirstein, once called the vaudeville circuit of this time the closest thing the United States had to a national school for the performing arts. That schooling ended for Lew and Harold in the summer of 1934, when while on tour in New York with their variety dance act they were invited to join the extravagant operetta *The Great Waltz*.

It was an amazing time to be a young dancer in New York, particularly an American ballet dancer, just as this identity was about to achieve legitimacy at home. The School of American Ballet, headed by Balanchine, had opened officially in January 1934. By fall Harold and Lew were studying there regularly, performing at night and taking class during the day. Lew would later sardonically comment that *The Great Waltz* was a total waste of time artistically. The value lay in making it possible for him to discover Balanchine. Through Balanchine's class Lew also met fellow student Gisella Caccialanza, protégée of the great Italian ballet teacher Enrico Cecchetti. Lew and Gisella would marry in 1941.

Within a few months both Christensen brothers and their dance partners had contracts with the Metropolitan Opera Ballet, where Balanchine had been appointed ballet master in early 1935. The pay was constant but so was the low regard for dancers. The Met treated the dancers like serfs, commanding them to serve as supernumeraries when needed, and forbidding them from watching the singers from the wings and from taking elevators to their crowded fourth-floor dressing rooms. The elevators were reserved for the star opera singers.

The Metropolitan Opera Ballet, however, provided the first occasion for Balanchine's Ballets Russes choreography, the 1928 *Apollon Musagète*, to be danced by the new American danseur Lew Christensen. Balanchine took Lew's well-proportioned muscularity and lankiness and turned it into a more extended line, and he highlighted Lew's musicality and phrasing and displayed his prodigious technique. Balanchine called Lew's multiple pirouettes the cleanest he ever saw, and Kirstein spoke for himself and Balanchine when, on the occasion of that 1936 restaging, he lauded Lew for dancing the best Apollo they had witnessed. That same year Lew also danced the lead in the premiere of Balanchine's *Orpheus and Eurydice*. Again his athletic, elegant, and unmannered style won over the critics, Balanchine, and especially Kirstein. "It was how Lew danced on stage and behaved off that signified to me a future, and within it a potential for American male dancers," Kirstein said admiringly. In 1936 he would bankroll a small touring ensemble, Ballet Caravan, featuring Lew as a principal dancer and choreographer of one of the first ballets on a contemporary American subject, the 1938 *Filling Station*. Now that Kirstein had his prize American danseur, he wanted to help cultivate his American choreographic voice as well.

Tragically, however, in less than six years, when Lew was thirty-two, his dancing career would effectively be over. On November 11, 1942, at the height of his performing ability and successful Ballet Caravan tours, and the start of a promising choreographic career, Lew was inducted into the United States Army. Having started out on such a high level of accomplishment and by having his career cut short by active military duty in a time of war, Lew assumed a mythic identity in the dance world. For an American public still worried about ballet feminizing men, he embodied a romantic narrative of the new macho American danseur who could hold a ballerina in one arm and a semi-automatic rifle in the other.

Lincoln Kirstein only added to the narrative saga of Lew's heroic manliness when he wrote about running into Lew driving a jeep on a European battlefield during World War II. Kirstein described how Lew had been assigned to the most traumatic of war duties, picking up corpses and pieces of flesh after the battles. After Lew returned to the United States following four years in the infantry, his muscles never regained their former elasticity and strength. Jocelyn Vollmar, who danced with San Francisco Ballet for more than 25 years, recalls performing *Swan Lake* with Christensen in 1950 and being aware of the physical frustrations he must have been feeling. "He still seemed very fine to me," she says. "He hung in there." He had given a short but dazzling prelude to American ballet, championing quiet strength and classical grace as companion manly attributes.

Meanwhile, Willam, always practical, had gotten himself and the best dancers from his family's Portland dance school hired to perform in the 1937 San Francisco Opera Ballet season. Borrowing brothers Lew and Harold as guest artists, he had next impressed Merola with his ballet instruction and choreography in a special performance at the Women's City Club of Oakland and the East Bay on September 17, 1937. It was a covert audition for the position of ballet master and it worked.

By the start of the fall 1938 season, the Christensen legacy at San Francisco Opera Ballet had officially begun. Willam would direct the ballet for the next fourteen years, initiating active touring and a vastly expanded repertory, while his brother Harold ran the school and tightened finances. In May 1942 Willam and Harold purchased the ballet school and company from the San Francisco Opera for $900. Mrs. Mark L. McDonald, the opera board member most sympathetic to the ballet, arranged the meeting with the brothers and representatives of the opera. Just as the opera was about to discontinue the ballet as a wartime cost-saving measure, this purchase meant instead that the word *opera* disappeared from the title.

Over the next few years Lew began the first of several visits as a guest choreographer and dancer for the company while serving as ballet master of New York City Ballet with Balanchine. Harold directed the San Francisco Ballet School until he was pressured to retire in 1975, as his failing health slowed him. In 1952, Willam moved with his family back to Utah, where he would start a ballet program at the University of Utah, and Lew assumed the full directorship of the San Francisco Ballet company, spending the next thirty-two years working for its growth and at times its simple survival throughout a rapidly changing landscape for dance in the United States.

Growth and Its Challenges

In 1963 the company was awarded a sizable $644,000 grant from the Ford Foundation, under the leadership of foundation vice president W. McNeil Lowry, as part of an unprecedented program of funding for the nation's leading ballet companies in an effort to stabilize them and their schools. Where once aesthetic concerns mattered most, now financial solvency was important too. Relations with the opera were also problematic, reinforcing Lew's lifelong dislike of opera management since his experiences at the Met. Merola's successor, the Austrian conductor Kurt Herbert Adler displayed little regard for ballet, often cutting choreography in last-minute rehearsals and prompting the ballet to look elsewhere for paid performances. In 1942 the opera and ballet had formally separated, and the opera created its own opera ballet, a seasonal pick-up company of mostly local dancers and commissioned choreography.

Lew had been looking for a partner to share the directorship of the company, and early in 1973 he flew to New York to audition new dancers and confer with Michael Smuin, who had trained with Willam, danced with San Francisco Ballet in the 1950s, and was now a principal dancer and choreographer with American Ballet Theatre. Smuin, thirty-four, who also had experience with popular dancing, having toured in a nightclub act with his wife, Paula Tracy, agreed to become San Francisco Ballet's new associate director. Some saw the partnership as "a marriage of opposites" because of Smuin's brassy style and showy choreography. Lew, however, spoke optimistically about creating a new look for the company. "Now we're going to build up a relationship like that of Balanchine and Robbins or Petipa and Ivanov in St. Petersburg," he told a dance writer. As Lew's health declined, Smuin was elevated to co-director in 1976, continuing until just after Lew's death in 1984 and the appointment of Helgi Tomasson as the company's new artistic director.

In 1974, after several costly new productions, including premieres in 1973 of a lavish full-length ballet, Lew and Smuin's *Cinderella,* and Lew's one-act *Don Juan,* San Francisco Ballet was deeply in debt. Many on the company's board of trustees favored declaring bankruptcy and disbanding the company—two ideas that were anathema to Lew. Instead, dancers and some trustees launched a citywide Save Our Ballet campaign. Dancers performed in storefronts, at amusement parks, and in the street, rallying public support and attracting enough funds to avoid dissolution. A dramatically updated new organizational structure followed, replacing a system that was almost unchanged since Willam started the company in 1942.

A consultant was hired, and at his recommendation, Richard LeBlond Jr., an academic and arts administrator, began in January 1975 as the ballet's first full-time paid president and general manager. LeBlond developed the company's first professional fund-raising program and five-year plan, strategizing how to regain the financial trust of funders and erase the debt. Within two years San Francisco Ballet was solvent, and Lew found that for the first time he could make new ballets without worrying about funding. The phase when ballet companies were headed and operated by their founding artistic professionals was passing. Increasingly companies everywhere needed leadership with administrative and financial expertise.

Today, decades after the company's beginning, Artistic Director Helgi Tomasson has created a new company identity that fuses the American aesthetic attributes of speed and energized attack with the elegance and technical purity of older European ballet traditions. In the twenty-first century, Americanization in ballet is about hybrids. In place of a fiercely defined and defended Americanness, an extraordinary variety of classical ballet traditions mix in the studios and stages of San Francisco Ballet. The company's outstanding foreign-born dancers during the later years of Tomasson's tenure include Gonzalo Garcia, Pascal Molat, Damian Smith, Gennadi Nedvigin, and Yuan Yuan Tan as well as Muriel Maffre and Yuri Possokhov. All provide a rich counterpart to equally impressive American-trained principal dancers like Joanna Berman, David Palmer, Katita Waldo, Kristin Long, Evelyn Cisneros, and Stephen Legate.

At the three-quarter-century mark, this ballet globalism stretches into the artistic ranks of the company and school. Tomasson has strengthened and reintroduced world influences by bringing in dancers and choreographers of international training and heritage and by touring the company regularly to major European capitals. At the same time, the company maintains its mission of presenting ballet as a rich medium of contemporary expression for the broad American public, positioning classical ballet as a critical part of this cosmopolitan city's cultural life. The teaching and artistic staff, dancers, and repertory are all international. San Francisco Ballet speaks ballet with many accents. Yet the body language is unmistakably contemporary, a democracy of classicism that began with the start of American ballet, in San Francisco, seventy-five years ago.

30) Joanna Berman and Vadim Solomakha in Harald Lander's *Etudes* (1998)

31) Tiit Helimets and Nutnaree Pipit-Suksun in David Bintley's *The Dance House* (2006)

33) Helgi Tomasson choreographing (1988)

2

34–35) Company class
on the Opera House
stage (2005)

36) (left to right) Ruby
Asquith Christensen
(Harold's wife),
Leon Kalimos (past
San Francisco Ballet
general manager),
Lew Christensen,
Harold Christensen,
Gisella Caccialanza
Christensen (Lew's wife),
and Willam Christensen
at the groundbreaking
ceremony of the
San Francisco Ballet
building (1982)

More than a Building

On the sunny afternoon of May 17, 1982, seventy-three-year-old
Lew Christensen took a shovel and dug it into the rocky dirt on an empty
corner lot behind the War Memorial Opera House. As his brothers Willam and
Harold stood by his side, Lew lifted the spade full of earth and the assembled
crowd cheered. This antique shovel was the same spade that had been used
for the groundbreaking of the Golden Gate Bridge in 1933, the year of San
Francisco Ballet's founding. Symbolically, the construction project that Lew's
gesture commenced would be a bridge of another sort—a vital span between
the past and the future of the ballet. Helping Lew hold the shovel aloft for
photographers was Richard LeBlond Jr., who as president and chief executive
officer of the ballet represented the increasingly important financial and
administrative side of the company.

After choreography and artistic leadership, the most fundamental resource
for a ballet company is its home. This houses the studios in which the dancers
take daily class, learn new roles, participate in the creation of new ballets,
rehearse, and essentially spend all their nonperforming working hours.
Space for dancers is a critical companion of the art form. It frames and invites
the scale of their movements and the velocity and line of their actions.
The space in which dancers work shapes the kind of story their dancing can
tell. Buildings also display stories about the institutions housed within them—
reflecting stability, stature, and prominence. Particularly with a "product"
as ephemeral as dance, theaters and home buildings are among a company's
few permanent markers.

The Ballet's Homes

The history of San Francisco Ballet's rise to excellence in the last quarter century is a story encapsulated in the building that has been its home since 1983, and the community of forces that sustain it.

In 1952, soon after Lew took over the directorship from Willam, San Francisco Ballet moved to Eighteenth Avenue in the residential San Francisco neighborhood known as the Richmond District, several miles from the Opera House. There, using bonds Harold had purchased over the years with the proceeds from the company's school, they acquired a two-story parking garage and converted it into three studios with offices below. Eventually, when a fourth studio was built downstairs, three apartments up the street were rented for the administrative staff, who had to use the ovens in the apartment kitchens to store papers as the organization continued to grow. When the company initially moved to Eighteenth Avenue, the setting had seemed spacious for what was then a small ensemble of eighteen dancers. Over time, however, the building became outdated and overcrowded. Ceilings were low, and the two showers and toilets had to be shared by what had grown to fifty dancers in the company in addition to the scores of children in the school. The company's co-director at the time, Michael Smuin, said that when the dancers performed in theaters he could practically see them reflexively duck whenever they were lifted because they were so accustomed to hitting their heads on the low ceilings and pipes in the studios. The company's earlier homes had been even more makeshift—the basement of an old hotel, the second floor of a lodge hall (where company member Jocelyn Vollmar remembers water pouring through the ceiling onto the studio floor every time it rained), and a small theater on Washington Street between Polk Street and Van Ness Avenue.

Finances could be equally tenuous. James J. Ludwig, president of the board of trustees in the 1960s, recalls how critical the early board support was. "I used to call Harold [Zellerbach, a trustee] just about every Friday and say, 'Harold, we don't have enough money to meet the payroll.' And Harold never let us down." Other problems might be resolved through strategic business lunches. Ludwig recounts that during this period when the company was presenting its seasons in the Geary Theatre, company manager Leon Kalimos casually mentioned to a reporter one day that the backstage area was a firetrap. "Louis Lurie, who owned the theater, read this and was in a rage," Ludwig says. "So Harold Zellerbach and I went down and had lunch with Louis at Jack's and solved that for the time being." In the early 1970s, Stephen A. Zellerbach followed in his father's footsteps. As chair of the board, he made the decision to put the association in debt guaranteed by members of the board as a way to foster the company's reputation and to re-establish its permanent home at the Opera House. As the scale of the company grew, so did the scope of its problems and style of their resolution.

In 1983, after thirty-one years, San Francisco Ballet was finally returning to the neighborhood where it had begun, but as a dramatically expanded, and financially much more stable, enterprise. This journey back to a home address next door to the Opera House symbolized a significant evolution in the life of the company and, equally profoundly, the board of trustees and the community. "San Francisco compared to some other places is very small," longtime trustee Lucy Jewett notes of the double challenge historically of raising money for the ballet in San Francisco. "But we have a number of enormously generous people who have gotten us where we are today."

Representatives of the ballet, headed by Philip Schlein, chair of the board from 1978 to 1982, had worked with city officials to acquire the site for the new building from the San Francisco Redevelopment Agency. A smaller adjacent lot that held an old gas station owned by the Union Oil Company was obtained directly from the president of Union Oil, Fred Hartley, after LeBlond, Ludwig, and L. Jay Tenenbaum, campaign chair, traveled to Los Angeles to take the Union Oil executive and his wife and daughter to dinner and a performance of San Francisco Ballet at the University of California at Los Angeles. "They loved the performance," Ludwig says. "We worked out a deal where Union Oil gave us half of the property and the other half we purchased for half of the appraisal."

Tenenbaum, an executive with the global investment banking firm of Goldman Sachs, together with LeBlond headed a $13.8 million fund-raising campaign to create a custom-designed building for the ballet on this land, cushioned with an endowment to maintain it. Tenenbaum cites project manager Mike Abramson as critical to the planning of the interior, delivering to the Ballet a $15 million building for $13.8 million. The neighborhood had yet to undergo redevelopment and was a trouble-prone area with no restaurants or small businesses. In a cheering repeat of the kind of grassroots community support that had helped build the Opera House, nearly nine hundred individuals gave personal contributions to the building fund, supplementing the corporate and foundation grants. Fritz and Lucy Jewett, Thomas J. Perkins, and the Rudolph W. Driscolls were major donors. A modest $300,000 grant from the National Endowment for the Arts for a 1980 feasibility study was the only federal money used in any part of the project.

The four-story concrete and glass building designed by San Francisco architect and ballet subscriber Beverly Willis was deliberately planned to look modest from the street, with the amenities and details like soothing pastel-painted walls and trompe l'oeil images of shady walkways painted on the interior hallways. It was the first structure in the nation built specifically to house all the operations of a professional dance company. Ballet buildings around the world were studied as models, and San Francisco Ballet dancers were interviewed about their needs over a two-year design and planning phase.

Less than two years after the ground-breaking, the doors of the state-of-the-art San Francisco Ballet building opened on December 17, 1983, with a series of festivities for the press, donors, and public. With this move to the new building at 455 Franklin Street, the ballet took its place alongside the city's other anchor arts institutions, including the opera, the symphony, and, until its move to new quarters in 1995, the San Francisco Museum of Modern Art. Lew Christensen was overwhelmed by the expansiveness of the new building: the nine big sunlit studios with twelve- to fifteen-foot ceilings, custom sprung floors, and acoustical panels to reduce music reverberation; the library; the audiovisual facilities; the board room; the physical therapy center; and the spacious locker rooms for the dancers. He told the press that the building meant one thing—"it said in concrete 'San Francisco Ballet is here to stay.'"

39) The San Francisco Ballet building (2006)

Endurance was only a small part of what the building signified. Most dramatically, it signaled the extraordinary new resources of financial support for the ballet from the trustees and the local community and a new esteem for the dancers as professionals. "I certainly hope the new building will say something more about the dancers being adults," said LeBlond, the administrative steward of the San Francisco Ballet Association at the time. "I think that when you give dancers a professional building to work in instead of a schlock environment, their professional dignity is bound to be affected. That's been a long time coming in the ballet world where dancers are still repellently referred to as 'boys and girls.'"

Metaphorically, the completion of the new building would be a profound marker of the artistic potential of San Francisco Ballet and its return, literally and figuratively, to the heart of the city's civic life. It was an occasion that was unimaginable just a decade earlier when the ballet had been at its lowest point financially, teetering on the edge of bankruptcy. Then, as the opera and symphony's homes were expanded, the ballet had been deliberately left out of the new spaces for the city's leading arts organizations. Lucy Jewett, who joined the board of trustees in 1969 soon after moving to San Francisco with her husband, says she and other board members were sure the company was going to close down in the mid-1970s, as its financial problems were so staggering. The dancers and some savvy board members, including Rudolph W. Driscoll and R. Stanley Dollar Jr., had decided to take the crisis to the streets. Dubbing their efforts Save Our Ballet (SOB), they staged the company's need in the most dramatic way possible by having dancers in tutus on street corners, in storefront windows, and on the backs of elephants at a local theme park to publicize the company's plight.

In many ways the building anticipated San Francisco Ballet's changing identity. Perhaps coincidentally, the first two years in it were among the most tumultuous in the company's history and, in retrospect, also the most portentous. In less than a year the Christensen era would be over with the sudden death of Lew from a heart attack in October 1984. A few months later Smuin's tenure with the ballet would also end, after a contentious and protracted public battle over the company's future direction.

Today the only public marker of that period, beyond the building itself, is the fifteen-foot, pale green commemorative wall in the ground-floor lobby of the ballet building. There, carved into the glass in silver letters, are the names of the hundreds of individual, corporate, and foundation donors whose contributions raised the building. Only five former dancers remain who danced in the old studios under the previous directors—Ballet Mistresses Betsy Erickson and Anita Paciotti, Principal Character Dancer and Choreographer Val Caniparoli, School Administrative Manager Jim Sohm, and Ballet Master Ricardo Bustamante. The building itself has been expanded with the addition of an annex in 2004—four floors of office space and a conference room to house the expanding marketing and fund-raising divisions. In addition, dance studios were refurbished. The break room for dancers was expanded, locker rooms updated, and a Wellness Center with weight machines and Pilates equipment added. Studio space for the ballet school was also expanded. The dainty trompe l'oeil wall paintings have vanished, replaced by vivid photographs of the dancers in the excitement of midperformance and rehearsals.

A Day in the Life of the Ballet Building

The most valued and lovingly tended interior real estate in the building are the dance studios. Each weekday morning as the building slowly awakens just before 7 A.M., Todd Martin, facility assistant, walks through the nine studios spread among the first and fourth floors. He systematically checks for any accidental leaks from the ventilation system or skylights onto the cherished floors where the dancers of the company and the students in the school train, rehearse, and spend their working lives.

Unlocking doors as he moves through the stairwells, corridors, offices, and locker rooms, Martin pauses to monitor the water quality in the company's third-floor spa, where the dancers soak their fatigued and sore muscles at the day's end in a large Jacuzzi. Turning on the fan and heating system in each studio, lights, computers, and coffee machines, he makes his rounds in forty-five minutes, ending back at the front reception desk just as the man responsible for cleaning, repairing, and tenderly conditioning the studio floors, Andy Bretthaur, is winding down. With skills as nuanced as those of a piano tuner, and more precious, Bretthaur is a master of self-cultivated expertise. For nearly thirty years, starting in the company's old home on Eighteenth Avenue, he has worked nightly between 1 A.M. and 9 A.M. removing dirt, water, sweat, and, if horn players have been practicing in the rooms, even spittle from the studio floors.

Between 8:30 A.M. and 9:30 A.M. the administrative offices on the third floor begin filling with staff. Executive Director Glenn McCoy, who is responsible for the broadest administrative view at the company, spends much of his day focused on board development and fund-raising with the trustees. The affable McCoy, who worked his way through the ballet's administrative levels beginning as assistant to the general manager, places a high value on consensus building and team problem solving. "I ask for people to weigh in on issues that aren't necessarily in their silo," he says in his soft southern accent.

A few doors away, General Manager Lesley Koenig oversees what she calls the art behind the dance, by managing the departments that make dance onstage possible. "There's art everywhere here, in the costume shops and the shops where we build and paint scenery, in the makeup and wig rooms, in the props, sound, and lighting departments, in the orchestra pit, and onstage where the stagehands make the work behind the magic of theater look effortless," Koenig says. "I negotiate and manage the labor contracts of all seven unions and oversee our four facilities and touring. I try to make Helgi's visions plastic, real, material, and affordable. I am responsible for spending most of the money at the ballet. My job is never, ever boring."

McCoy's and Koenig's offices are just down the hall from Artistic Director Helgi Tomasson's office in what is known as the "artistic" suite of offices, one floor below the fourth-floor company studios. McCoy, who has been with the ballet since 1987, says that when things get stressful he slips upstairs to peek in a studio and remind himself of the extraordinary beauty that is the point of his and his staff's labors.

The crew of the Wellness Center trickles in next. The second-floor offices, headquarters for the San Francisco Ballet School and Dance in Schools and Community program, start coming to life around 9:30 A.M. when the class for the trainees begins. These select advanced students are being given one year of special technical polishing for professional dance careers before being taken into San Francisco Ballet or another professional company. By 11 A.M. the second-floor hallways are cluttered with the backpacks, dance bags, and reclining bodies of students stretching. These are the advanced students in the school, fourteen- and fifteen-year-olds who cram in a half day of academic work in the morning and then race to the ballet for afternoon classes and rehearsals that continue into the early evening. A sign on the first floor reminds the students to use the stairs between the first and second floors in order to keep the elevators open for the dancers in the company. From the moment they walk through the locked doors past the lobby, even the youngest dancer is taught the system of status that surrounds ballet and the courtesy and deference that a dancer accrues as she advances in rank through the school and company.

The fourth floor, where the company's studios are located, is the last level of the building to come to life. Many of the dancers arrive in advance of the 10 A.M. daily company class so they can chat and leisurely stretch or sip juice before their day begins. At the height of the season, daily classes, rehearsals, and performances can fill nine or ten hours. Wherever and whenever the company is working, the activity is always grounded with the ritual of class each morning. When the ballet is in rehearsal but not performing, company class is usually held in the Christensen Studio, the biggest room in the building and a space that matches the dimensions of the Opera House stage. The exceptions are days when the men and women are given separate classes and drilled in the repertory of steps distinct to each sex. Once the season begins, company

class is often held on the Opera House stage. Sometimes if there is a particularly challenging musical work in the repertory, Michael McGraw, company pianist, might be in the Christensen Studio before the dancers arrive, having come in earlier to practice on the grand piano that is used for accompanying class and often rehearsals too, if they are done to a piano reduction of the score.

Company class and rehearsals are among the most private times of the day for the dancers. This is when they prepare to be seen, what former company principal Stephen Legate once called "the ninety-nine percent of our lives when we are preparing for the one percent of our lives when we are actually onstage performing." Ballet Masters Ashley Wheater and Ricardo Bustamante, both former leading dancers with the company, alternate with another former principal dancer, Joanna Berman, and Helgi Tomasson, in teaching company class. Each one's style is a bit different as they relay indirectly the nuances of their attributes as dancers onto the absorbent bodies of the company—Tomasson's impeccable classicism, Berman's buoyant musicality, Wheater's elegant line, Bustamante's weighted attack. But the end result is the same: to prepare each dancer's body, respectfully, systematically, and insistently, to perform to the highest level of its potential and with a spirited individuality.

Oftentimes, some of the trainees from the ballet school will slip upstairs during breaks in their own classes and watch through the open door or, if the studio doors are closed, through the small viewing window in each door. The boys in particular will cheer a favorite male dancer in the fast-turning fouetté competitions that customarily end class. For anyone else not directly a part of the ballet organization, watching class, and particularly rehearsals, is usually strictly prohibited.

Immediately after class, the dancers check the rehearsal schedule posted in the hall for any last-minute changes (most have already viewed it the night before online) and file into the studios to begin the long afternoon of rehearsals. Complex, and paradoxical, webs of privacy and display surround ballet companies. The dancers spend ten hours a day preparing to be visible while striving to be invisible in the process. In essence they are continually practicing to be seen, perfecting actions behind closed doors, with their fellow dancers as the only witnesses, until they are ready to go before the public and revel in being seen as their bodies and actions are scrutinized by thousands. In class and rehearsal, the wall of floor-to-ceiling mirrors in each studio takes the place of this audience, reflecting back to the dancers an image they are always trying to surpass.

The Littlest Dancers

As the afternoon wears on, the downstairs lobby begins to fill with the noisy chatter and undisciplined bodies of the youngest dancers in the building, the five- and six-year-old preballet students. As the public school day ends, the ballet school day begins, and by 4 P.M. every sofa in the lobby is filled with parents and siblings waiting for the aspiring dancer in the family to finish class. The very smallest students go no farther than the first floor where six-year-olds take once-a-week preballet class from Kristi DeCaminada, who is warm and encouraging yet conveys clear standards. Meeting them in the lobby, she walks them down the hall to the Jewett Studio, where she introduces them to the five cardinal foot positions of classical ballet from which they will begin and end practically every ballet movement they will do for the rest of their dancing lives.

42-43) The San Francisco
Ballet School's preballet
students (2006)

44) Trainees and students
in levels seven and eight
(2006)

45) Trainees and level
eight students rehearsing
(2006)

TRAINING FOR GLORY
(AND HEARTBREAK)

The most desired leap, and often the most perilous, for any young dancer is the move from student to company member. Starting in fall 2005, that journey became a bit more predictable for the twelve fortunate young ballet students in the inaugural class of the San Francisco Ballet Trainee Program. Conceived by Artistic Director Helgi Tomasson and coordinated by Leslie Young, a former San Francisco Ballet soloist, the trainee program takes an international group of highly promising sixteen- to nineteen-year-olds, selected from the advanced summer session, and saturates them in a full-time program structured around the rarely taught skills for getting hired and surviving as a dancer.

"Helgi's vision is that this program is the step between the school and the company," Young says. "The hope is that this one-year window will really give the trainees the strength for all that lies ahead—technically and psychologically." Among the skills a sixteen-year-old petite and vivacious dancer from Japan and an eighteen-year-old from Israel were drilled in was how to go through what Young calls "heartbreak."

"I teach them that when they go to audition they need to understand the bigger picture," she says. "It's not just about 'Do they like me? Am I good enough?'" Young explains that being a good fit with a company has to do with many other factors. "We've all been through this, where you feel like you've just been stabbed when you are rejected. So I tell them they have to look at the bigger picture. If they are rejected, it's just that they aren't right at this time. Maybe a five-foot-ten dancer just left. Will hiring a five-foot-four dancer fill that?"

The approach Young teaches the trainees, all of whom are on tuition scholarships, favors research as well as physical preparation. Believing that auditioning well is a skill set, as is choosing potential companies wisely, Young assigns each trainee to research ballet companies and look at the repertory, the directors, and videos of the performances. "I want them to be intelligent dancers who have a vision," she says. Part of that vision is to build the young dancers' confidence. "I want each of them to find a way to work positively," Young says. "I think as dancers we have such a tendency to beat ourselves up. You're your worst critic and you get to a point where you think, 'Ugh! I'm horrible.' When you get to that point, no work gets done because you are too discouraged to try."

The trainees get passes to the San Francisco Ballet season, and Young also takes them to the symphony, museums, and the opera. "It's not an easy transition from student to company member, but this is the point at which you decide your life in art is real. You are ready to put on blinders for dance, and in the process open up the world," she says. For Diego Cruz, an animated nineteen-year-old from Spain, the "real"—his life as a professional artist—began just as the trainee year ended and he received a contract as one of the newest members of San Francisco Ballet's corps de ballet.

46) San Francisco Ballet students perform August Bournonville's *Konservatoriet* at Student Showcase (2006)

47) Students in George Balanchine's *Stars and Stripes* at Student Showcase (2005)

47

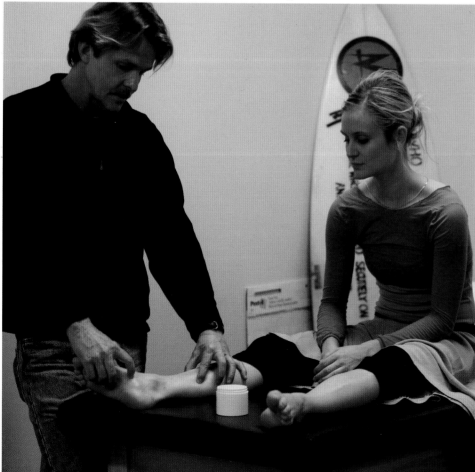

48–49) San Francisco Ballet
students in a performance
of Helgi Tomasson's
Nutcracker (2005)

50–51) The corps de ballet
rehearses Helgi Tomasson's
Swan Lake (2005)

52 t) Ballet Mistress
Betsy Erickson and
Katita Waldo take a break
between rehearsals
(2006)

52 b) Company Physical
Therapist Michael Leslie
works with Elizabeth Miner
in the Wellness Center
(2006)

53) Lorena Feijoo and
Davit Karapetyan
rehearse Helgi Tomasson's
Swan Lake (2006)

After one or two years of study, the students progress to the second floor of the ballet building, where they will spend the next eight to ten years of their preprofessional existence, working their way up to levels seven and eight, the most advanced classes in the San Francisco Ballet School. The move from this second floor of the school to the fourth-floor company classes and rehearsals can take a young lifetime, and sometimes it never happens. At 455 Franklin Street, the highest level in the building is the highest level in the art form.

There is logic but also paradox here. Professional ballet is an institution with age inversion. The ones being attended to are the young; older people serve them. It is the attributes of youth that are continually celebrated in ballet—speed, daring, elevation, and boundless energy. But they take the fiercely disciplined and focused mind of an adult to accomplish, and all of this needs to be packaged in bodies of great beauty, ideal physicality, and strength.

The Ballet's Support Groups

Several nights each month, a more public life in the building commences in the late afternoon and early evening. These are the times when the ballet's support wings in the community gather. The board of trustees, as well as the San Francisco Ballet Auxiliary, ENCORE!, and BRAVO (Ballet Resources and Volunteer Organization), the company's three volunteer support organizations, hold their regular meetings in the first-floor Dollar Board Room, named after 1960s trustee and donor R. Stanley Dollar Jr.

For the majority of board members, however, it is their deeds rather than their names that endure. James H. Herbert II, trustee and board chair since 2002 and co-chair with Pamela Joyner since 2006, says it is people's interest in the art form that first and finally binds them to San Francisco Ballet. Like board chairs Chris Hellman and J. Stuart Francis before him, Herbert has worked steadily to diversify the donor base, not just the donations to the company. "You have to get people interested in the art form," he says of his philosophy of growing supporters of the ballet. "At the end of the day if they aren't interested in the art form they won't give to the arts." That outlook has been the foundation of what Executive Director Glenn McCoy calls the sophisticated approach to financing that Herbert introduced to the ballet. "Jim Herbert has brought a much more diversified way of financing to the ballet so that we have not just an ambitious annual fund but also a campaign to get the endowment to $100 million and special bond issues to support facilities enhancement and the creation of new work." Unprecedented in the ballet's history, this support has made possible the purchase of a vintage Victorian home as a dormitory for twenty-six students in the school and a warehouse to consolidate the storage of the company's costumes and sets from four scattered smaller warehouses. "My objective in a final sense is to capitalize on Helgi's brilliance," Herbert says. "To institutionalize the current success and his legacy. People really like to be part of excellence," he continues, turning the focus back to the company's achievement as the true generator of donations.

Among the many partnerships that it takes to sustain the company, the San Francisco Ballet Auxiliary has the most fun as it stages elegant social affairs throughout the season. Beginning with the lavish gala dinner in the City Hall Rotunda at the commencement of the season and continuing to the annual fashion show and supper before the student showcase performances toward the end of the season in early May, the Auxiliary creates occasions for supporters of San Francisco Ballet to have a good time while raising serious money—more than $1 million annually—for the company. The Auxiliary has evolved into a powerful women-only organization that caps its membership at one hundred, with numerous hopefuls waiting to be sponsored to join when a vacancy opens. In many respects, the Auxiliary and the board of trustees are the cultural, social, and civic faces of San Francisco Ballet. Through social occasions that can be as choreographed, costumed, and carefully timed as a dance, the Auxiliary represents the ballet to the community and in turn brings the city's civic leaders to the ballet. There is a historical dimension to this relationship as well because the board and Auxiliary link San Francisco Ballet to the old European and Russian traditions of social patronage that have long wrapped professional ballet companies in the civic embrace of a community's business and social leaders.

Lisa Grotts, 2005–07 president of the Auxiliary, says that the gala dinner is about having a great time while contributing significant funds to the ballet. The elegant sit-down dinner for one thousand patrons is held in the grand marble rotunda, mezzanine, and North and South Light Courts of City Hall.

Wandering through the gala dinner was like time-traveling through a frame of the royal court of Louis XIV. The etiquette, ornateness, and ceremony suggested the rediscovery of the baroque moment when ballet was born—only now the city's "nobility" are defined by philanthropy rather than birth in an evening that mirrors a royal fete. Immediately after a meal prepared by the city's leading chefs, ballet patrons dash across the street to the Opera House for the gala performance that inaugurates the ballet season. In the downstairs hall of the Opera House, ENCORE!, a group of younger ballet enthusiasts and subscribers started in 1993, hosts its own fund-raising dinner. Vicariously, those bodies onstage become the audience's for the evening. The pleasures of making that possible are the reward that sustains the thousands who work, support, build, and watch San Francisco Ballet.

55) Opening Night Gala (2007)

3

Daily Company Class

Company class, the ritual that begins the day for every San Francisco Ballet dancer, is a rite of transformation. Standing at the barre at 10 A.M. every morning, the dancers work to wake up their bodies. They warm up their muscles and slowly coax tired limbs and joints, sore thighs, and swollen feet into sweeping extensions and crisply executed footwork so outside the range of what the body knows normally that it must be continually relearned. Class is where the dancers remember what they can do and learn to reach past what they cannot.

Although the dancers' actions are guided by whoever is teaching company class each day, nuances of individual styling open up almost immediately from the first *demi-pliés* at the barres. Muriel Maffre is quietly focused and thoughtful, testing the articulation of her feet one by one in a pair of worn pink toe shoes, which she trades out for sturdier pairs as the class progresses. Kristin Long favors deep thigh-stretching lunges as she stands at the "mommy barre," along with the other women principal dancers in the company who have children—Katita Waldo and Tina LeBlanc. Long, who joined the company in 1989 and has a nine-year-old son, says that the older dancers tend to group together in class so they might share "parent" news about things such as a glitch in childcare or a sick child home from school.

56–57) George Balanchine's
Who Cares? (2005)

58) Helgi Tomasson's
Giselle (2005)

Gonzalo Garcia, who in 2002 at age twenty-three became one of the youngest principal dancers in the company, works intently on a barre at the side of the room, repeatedly checking his line and position in the mirror as he executes each tautly stretched *tendu* with accute strength in his legs. What the other American male dancers in the corps good-naturedly refer to as "The Spanish Mafia," the Spanish-trained dancers in the company—Jaime Garcia Castilla, Moises Martin, Ruben Martin, and Dores Andre, along with the Cubans Joan Boada and Lorena Feijoo—collect at a barre near Garcia. Often, if Principal Dancers Pierre-François Vilanoba, Pascal Molat, or Nicolas Blanc are working near Muriel Maffre, soft asides in French can be heard between exercises at that part of the room. Kirov Ballet–trained Principal Dancer Gennadi Nedvigin works precisely and quietly; his legs shoot out and back with arrowlike rigor in swinging battements, which he executes with effortless efficiency. Tall and muscled Tiit Helimets, the Estonian-born principal dancer in the company, who joined in 2005, stretches his powerful legs with feet that curve fully with the arched beauty of a woman's foot in a pointe shoe.

Sometimes Lily Rogers, a willowy young corps member, will join a barre of principal dancers. "I find our principals, our soloists, even our senior corps members, extremely inspiring," Rogers says. "It was important to me to learn from them and to realize that I'm at the bottom all over again. I had worked my way up through the San Francisco Ballet School where I was at the top. Now overnight I'm a tiny fish in a really big sea. But the nice thing about this company is that there is always a place for the new person."

There is no strict hierarchy to the room or the socializing within the company— a rare thing in the professional ballet world. "There is a unity here you cannot find anywhere else," agrees Principal Dancer Pascal Molat. "I have performed with several companies in Europe, and I never saw a huge company with seventy people creating a sense of unity like this. Principals can speak with the corps and get advice from them. There is no star system here." Indeed, early on in his tenure as artistic director, Helgi Tomasson made a number of subtle changes in the company to help lessen precisely this creation of a "star" mentality among the dancers and the audiences. In his first year he ranked the dancers, designating them corps de ballet, soloists, and principal dancers. This didn't restrict what they could dance so much as formalize what he saw as their role and potential within the company and the expectations he had of their ability. After that, the custom of allowing fans in the audience to step to the front of the orchestra and hurl flowers at their favorite dancers during curtain calls was eliminated, replaced by formal bouquets supplied by the ballet that are presented onstage to dancers who have performed in a featured role on an opening night or gala. While this takes away a certain spontaneity on the part of the audience, it also puts the emphasis back on the premiere of new choreography at least as much as the individuals performing it.

Although it is only class, the pull of a performance is just behind and ahead of each morning's company class. With this comes the need for the instructor generally, and each dancer personally, to modulate the challenge and step up the demands. Class reflects the nature of the season's repertory. Joanna Berman, a popular dancer with the company for eighteen years beginning in 1984, began teaching company class regularly in 2003, a year after retiring and shortly before giving birth to twin boys. "Teaching company class is a unique challenge because you have seventy-five minutes to give each person the kind of training and work they need. You have young dancers who aren't dancing that much yet and need to work hard, and next to them are veterans with a very long day of demanding performing ahead," she explains. "So before class I try to ask a corps dancer and a principal and a soloist how they are doing to get a sense of what they feel is needed that day." In the ballet school, class creates the dancer; in the company, the repertory creates the class.

Teachers and Ballet Masters

The teacher is the pivotal force. One of the most beloved teachers at San Francisco Ballet during the first decade of Tomasson's tenure was Kirov-trained Irina Jacobson. The last protégée of the great Russian teacher Agrippina Vaganova, Jacobson was hired by Tomasson in 1987 to bring her impeccable sense of Russian classicism to company class and coaching as well as the advanced classes in the school. "Irina was so important here," says Garcia, who studied with Jacobson in the school and company until she left to work in Europe in 1997. "She came from that strict tradition of Vaganova where the classics are so well prepared in Russia, and at the same time she was a very open-minded person and realized that a young company with young dancers is going to dance the classics in a very different way. When I was in the school, she would teach 5 P.M. class with the girls. Sometimes I would finish my day and sneak in and take her class because I knew who she was. At first she didn't pay too much attention that I was there. They were very hard classes because the little girls have a lot of repetitions and have to hold one leg in the air a long time. I remember already being at the advanced level and thinking, 'God these classes are so hard,'" he laughs. "Once we were in a balance, and all the students were so in shape and well trained that they were like statues and wouldn't move. But I was tired and was just about to put my hand on the barre. I remember her suddenly shouting, 'Nooooo!' I had been thinking she was not paying attention to me, and she was screaming 'Nooooo! Don't even think about it!'"

60–61) George Balanchine's
Rubies (2006)

For Finnish-born Mikko Nissinen, who danced with San Francisco Ballet for ten years and now directs the Boston Ballet, Jacobson's presence at San Francisco Ballet and that of Tomasson were the inducements to his coming to the United States and San Francisco Ballet. "I heard Irina was going to be a full-time teacher with the company and so I thought, 'Well, Irina and Helgi . . . now it *was* time for me to come to America.' It was just meant to be."

Maintaining the dances in San Francisco Ballet's active repertory, and the artists who perform them, is among the most finely calibrated responsibilities in the company. This is essentially the job description of the ballet masters, and foremost among them are Ashley Wheater and Ricardo Bustamante, because they both teach company class. When Colombian-born Bustamante teaches, he likes to shape class to prime the company for the most demanding choreography of the moment. "I have a rule of thumb," says Bustamante, who danced with San Francisco Ballet and American Ballet Theatre, and also directed ballet companies in Chile and Buenos Aires, before Tomasson recruited him to return as ballet master in 2004. "If you think of class as only a warm-up, you might as well just go to the gym and get warm. Class is meant to improve your technique, improve the way you move, work on your expression, on your stage presence. So I make sure I give them a meaty class, so they can really have a good bite at it and yet be challenged on a gradual scale."

Ashley Wheater, Scottish born and trained at the Royal Ballet, does triple duty because he also serves as artistic assistant to Tomasson. Wheater, too, had a memorable career as a principal dancer with San Francisco Ballet and before that the Joffrey Ballet. He shares with Bustamante an awe for how the dancers of the current company are meeting technical challenges and demands that didn't exist in ballet even half a generation ago. "When we perform in London now, people say, 'Gosh the company can do anything,'" Wheater says. "They remark that you never see the women worry about going on pointe. You never see the men worrying about doing a double *tour* [turn]. They just fly through everything. The reason is that our dancers *are* that strong and they are taught to perform with that kind of delivery. When Helgi teaches class he demands from the dancers that they use technique to express themselves on a musical level and a level of being able to move freely. You need incredible technique to be able to do these things and you have to challenge yourself to carry out what he wants."

Bustamante sees the heightened demands in company class as the direct result of the demanding and diverse repertory that Tomasson has assembled during his tenure. "I think the invention and the creation of Helgi's season call for this nonstop process of stop-cutting-with-the-same-scissors and instead figure-out-what-everybody-needs approach," Bustamante says. "The choreographers are the biggest contributors to that. I'm just the mediator. For example, William Forsythe arrives for two days of rehearsals and the movement I am teaching in his ballet *Artifact Suite* has to have a ten, fifteen, twenty-inch *longer* line than what we were doing. The breath has to be bigger, the movement has to be bigger. Suddenly I've got to teach how to move differently and think much more ahead."

Even when technical demands were more modest, tailoring company class to the repertory has been a feature of San Francisco Ballet from its earliest days. Nancy Johnson Carter, a dancer with the company from 1944 to 1960 and administrative director of the school from 1986 to 1995, remembers that when Willam Christensen's choreography pandered unself-consciously to the audience, the styling in company class did, too. "If we were performing ballets that had more of a theatrical flavor, like Willam's version of *Coppélia* or his staging of *Swan Lake*, then his classes also became very theatrical," she says. "We would all be trained to make a strong finish and to *sell* whatever we were doing." When the leadership reins of the company shifted from Willam to Lew, a restyling of company class followed. Initially Lew's emphasis on a more rigorous technical and dramatically simpler technique and style of delivery, modeled on what he knew from Balanchine, puzzled the 1950s San Francisco Ballet dancers. "When Lew arrived we all thought everything was being reversed," Carter recalls with a laugh. "It became so precise and technical and cold." What Lew was introducing was an early model of Balanchine's evolving neoclassicism, which favored purity of line, clarity of intent, and speed. Tomasson's leadership of the company, along with the presence of New York City Ballet's Bonita Borne as ballet mistress during Tomasson's initial years, brought a reinfusion of this aesthetic, softened by the emerging pluralism of the repertory.

Company class reveals many things about a dancer. It is a portal to the company; once a dancer is in the company, it becomes the gateway to the stage and the roles one is given. Finally, for retired dancers like Bustamante, Wheater, and Berman, class is where they redefine their relationship to ballet and the company. "I remember before I taught company class for the first time Helgi talked with me," Berman says. "He told me about the need to have some separation because I had been a dancer with this company for so long and now I was coming over to the other side."

64 t) Ballet Master
Ricardo Bustamante
rehearses Helgi Tomasson's
Swan Lake with
Kristin Long (2006)

64 b) Ashley Wheater,
ballet master and assistant
to the artistic director,
in the studio (2006)

65) Katita Waldo
rehearses Helgi Tomasson's
The Sleeping Beauty (2000)

Class as Gateway to the Company

For the members of San Francisco Ballet, taking daily class is an expectation, and for former dancers, it is a job, but for those hoping to join the company, taking class is a nerve-racking high-stakes honor, an advanced placement and college entrance exam in one. When a dancer is interested in joining San Francisco Ballet, and usually after the artistic staff has viewed preliminary tapes, he or she is invited to take company class. Here, his or her fit with the company can be quietly appraised. French-born Pascal Molat, who joined the company in 2002, originally came to audition after hearing about the company in Europe and being impressed by the company's diverse repertory on the Web site.

"The class and the atmosphere in the class were so fantastic," he says enthusiastically. "But at the end of my audition I was doing the combination with two or three other men and accidentally I fell. At that moment the whole company suddenly began clapping!" Molat was stunned. Afterward Principal Dancer Joan Boada explained to Molat that this was the dancers' way of showing encouragement to dust off and try again. Molat was charmed. "I actually loved it," he says of the company and this ritual.

Australian-born Hayley Farr, a member of the corps, found herself penniless in Boston in 2004 while auditioning for American ballet companies, when Regina Bustillos, Tomasson's personal assistant, called and said that after viewing a video Farr had sent, Tomasson wanted her to come take class. When Farr haltingly explained that her wallet had just been stolen, the company flew her to San Francisco and put her up at the Inn at the Opera, the boutique hotel next door to the San Francisco Ballet building. "I couldn't believe they'd pay for this girl they'd never seen, just from a video, to come and stay," Farr says. "At the end of the week Helgi offered me a position in the corps. And then he gave me money out of his own pocket to get back to London!" Tomasson may well have remembered his own days as an aspiring young Icelandic dancer in New York, when he, too, had been penniless, without a job and days away from leaving the United States, and the Joffrey Ballet offered him a contract.

Muriel Maffre was dancing with the Ballets de Monte-Carlo, when she took class with San Francisco Ballet while the company was in Paris on tour in 1990. "At the time people were encouraging me to look to America because of the body that I have," says the tall, slender Maffre, who was offered a contract as a principal dancer after the audition. "I was impressed with the dancers because they had such a different way of dancing; the level of energy, the level of precision in the legwork. And I felt that there was a lot I could learn from them." For the first couple of years after joining the company, Maffre used class as a means to Americanize her dancing. "I was obsessed," she laughs. "I wanted to dance like an American dancer—directness, immediacy in the delivery. And this obsession brought me to the point where I realized it didn't work." The result for Maffre was to incorporate some of the new with how she had been dancing before that fateful company class.

Even when the company is on tour, company class can be at times like a big high school homeroom. It's the one time of the day when the whole company is together and where whimsical as well as serious information circulates. Typically, if it is a company member's birthday, the pianist launches into "Happy Birthday" at the end of class, and the dancers gather around the celebrant and applaud. This happened during the 2006 New York tour in the first class at the New York State Theatre, where the company was about to open in the Lincoln Center Festival that evening. Company class is also where Tomasson peeked his head in the door one morning in early April 2006 and quickly read the list of ballets for the coming season in a quiet voice to the suddenly hushed room. Then he disappeared back down the hallway, and the room erupted in speculative chatter.

Knowledge of what the company will be dancing in the forthcoming season is followed immediately by curiosity about who will get what coveted roles. "The company is so deep with talent, from the principals all the way to apprentices," Wheater says. "And that in itself challenges even the young ones." The apprentices are those on the cusp of becoming members of the company and transitioning out of the top-level classes in the school.

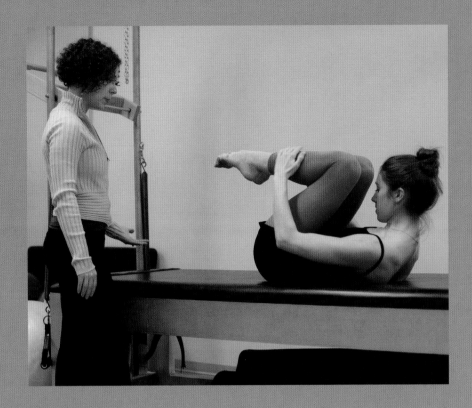

FEAR OF
NOT DANCING

Next to age, the specter that haunts dancers and threatens them with the loss of their life onstage is injury. When the San Francisco Ballet building opened in 1983, it featured what was then a state-of-the-art fitness center—an exercise bike, one set of free weights, and a part-time physical therapist. When it reopened after renovations in 2004, the center had a new name—the Wellness Center—and new facilities, including treadmills, recumbent bikes, climbing machines, a full Pilates studio, a jumbo Jacuzzi, and a massage room with a full- and a part-time physical therapist and a company chiropractor. The center also has seven consulting orthopedists as well as a medical supervisor, Dr. Richard Gibbs.

Located on the third floor, the Wellness Center has an entrance that intentionally crosses what Executive Director Glenn McCoy calls the invisible boundary that he discovered divides the artistic and administrative offices. "When we remodeled the building we tried to mix up the functions so we get to bump into the dancers and music staff more often," he says.

67) Rachel Viselli works
with a Pilates instuctor
in the Wellness Center
(2006)

The man with the wisest hands, Michael Leslie, company physical therapist, travels with the ballet whenever it tours. It's not unusual to see several dancers race up to him when he peeks his head in the company class in the morning, asking if he can work them in for a quick appointment before afternoon rehearsals. "Michael is invaluable because he has his hands on the dancers all the time," Medical Administrator Floriana Alessandria says. "The fear of every dancer is *not* dancing. So we make it as easy as possible for the dancers to stay able to work and heal without waiting for something to turn into a major injury. And they don't pay for a thing—we even buy their Band-Aids for them."

Choreographer Mark Morris commends San Francisco Ballet for its intelligent training and support of the dancers. "The dancers seem more vital. It's wonderful," Morris says. "The placement and stamina and cross-training or whatever they're doing—something is working."

"Yes, we are extremely spoiled," Gonzalo Garcia agrees. "We work with some of the best chiropractors, massage therapists . . . great acupuncture. When dancers' bodies are healthy, that's a success."

68) James Sofranko
and Muriel Maffre
rehearse Sir Kenneth
MacMillan's *Elite
Syncopations* (2002)

69) Corps de Ballet
men rehearsing
Jerome Robbins's
Glass Pieces (2006)

70) Rachel Viselli
before a performance
of Yuri Possokhov's
Reflections (2005)

71) Ruben Martin and
Sarah Van Patten in
Christopher Wheeldon's
Quaternary © (2006)

72) Yuri Possokhov
and Muriel Maffre in
Christopher Wheeldon's
Quaternary © (2006)

73) Tina LeBlanc
in George Balanchine's
*Harlequinade Pas
de Deux* (2006)

Young Students in Class

Yet even in the classes for the youngest students, the demands of the stage are evident as they prepare for the annual spring student showcase performances at the city's Palace of Fine Arts Theatre. At 6:45 P.M. on a Thursday in late March, when the rest of the San Francisco Ballet building has nearly emptied, Cuban-trained Jorge Esquivel, one of the company's principal character dancers and a teacher in the school since 1993, is drilling five slender boys in his level three class in the intricacies of *grand changement* and *sissonne* in preparation for this showcase. One boy, wearing puffy après-ski boots to keep his feet warm, watches from a chair next to the baby grand piano in the room. Esquivel, wearing all black and with his gray hair in a ponytail, pushes the boys to connect their torsos to their legs.

As they try repeatedly, Yoira Esquivel Brito, Esquivel's thirty-year-old daughter, peeks in, having just ended her class of level three girls in the studio next door. Prompted to comment by her father, she gently admonishes the boys to make more of their feet. "You don't have anything yet interesting in your faces, you are too young," she tells them. "So everyone will be looking at your feet." They try again, holding in their stomachs and pulling up through their legs as they spring rapidly in the air, crossing their feet sharply back and forth. Even in developing dancers this young, pushing into overtime at the end of a long day, the extraordinary reshaping—cognitively, emotionally, and physically—that it takes to ascend two flights to the company class in the big fourth-floor studio is evident.

Moving On: The Stage

The same tensions on the dancers in the studio—the need to transition from the prosaic body that might be sore, tired, or nervous into a flawless and confident performing medium—are compressed when the dancing moves to the Opera House stage. Here the constant flow from performing to not performing, from the lengthy hours of preparation to the few minutes of having it all come together in the lighted frame of the stage, become intense. Watching the corps de ballet in the second act of *Swan Lake* from the wings of the stage is like seeing a personality change every time a dancer steps off the brilliantly lit stage into the shadowy wings or from the wings back onto the stage. Onstage, the ensemble of twenty-four swans flows downstage in a dreamy serpentine path, balancing in arabesque as if floating on the glasslike surface of a pond. Shielding their faces with a softly curled arm, they pause in precise lines framing their swan queen Odette as if peeking from behind a soft-feathered wing. Yet when they exit and each swan in the ensemble crosses into the shadow of backstage, they drop off their pointes and bend over to rub a painful foot, or loosen the top hooks on a tight bodice as they dab at the sweat on their faces with tissues pulled from boxes ready in the wings.

Around the margins of the stage, an assortment of costume, makeup, production, electrical, lighting, property, and stage manager staff stand at the ready to quickly assist the needs of each ballet and the dancers, particularly the principal dancers and soloists, before they dash back onstage. Here the focused and articulate performing body is prepared for its brief time in the little lighted rectangle of the stage, surrounded by rings of the preparation, care, and technology that support it. "When you are dancing it's empowering," Muriel Maffre says. "But that sense of power is ephemeral so it's really a contradiction." There is no better vantage point to marvel at the evanescence of this power than the moment in the season when rehearsals move to the Opera House stage.

Among the things that are distinctive about Helgi Tomasson's tenure as artistic director of the company are the extra layers of transition he has built into this shift from the studios of the ballet building to the Opera House stage across the street. It is customary in most companies to have a single dress rehearsal just before opening night, but at San Francisco Ballet there are four or five separate rehearsals. A work-light staging rehearsal, sometimes two technical rehearsals, a full orchestra rehearsal with dancers, and a full dress rehearsal are each conducted on the Opera House stage. Mikko Nissinen says enviously that his own Boston Ballet "only has one full rehearsal before opening. It's about money," he mimes, rubbing the fingers of one hand together. Certainly there is an expense to every moment the ballet is in a fully staffed union theater like the Opera House, but for Tomasson there is also a determination about the standard of the finish that needs to be achieved before the curtain rises.

When the curtain finally falls at the conclusion of the evening, there is a brief flurry of ballet masters, ballet mistresses, and choreographers "giving notes" (quick comments about mistakes and successes) to the dancers in each ballet. Then, sometimes before the whole theater has even emptied, the curtain is raised as stagehands clear the stage, sweeping the soft vinyl floor covering clean as they push props to the side to make space for three rows of portable barres lined up across the depth of the stage. A small upright piano is rolled out from an upstage wing. The stage has become a classroom. It sits ready for the same glorious and physically exacting bodies that filled it only minutes earlier to return in the morning, tired, sore, and ready to push forward again in company class.

OFFSTAGE LESSONS

Damian Smith is stretched out on his stomach, his chin propped up on one palm as he reads in the dim light in a back corner of the Opera House stage. Around him, dancers dressed as nymphs, villagers, and slaves mark their entrances, chatting softly as they watch a rehearsal for the first act of Mark Morris's *Sylvia*. The elegant Australian-born principal dancer, in full costume and makeup as the ballet's evil, cave-dwelling hunter Orion, is preparing to write an analysis of one of Plato's allegories. In his early thirties and a dancer with San Francisco Ballet since 1996, Smith is at the top of his profession and at the beginning of his academic career.

Ten Sunday evenings during the company's season, after the matinee performance, Smith and thirteen other dancers shower, grab a snack, and dash over to a local hotel for four hours of classes where they are all students in a special college program, Liberal Education for Arts Professionals (LEAP). Founded in 1999 by Claire Sheridan, the visionary former dancer and teacher at Saint Mary's College of California, LEAP validates years of professional dancing as valuable life experience deserving of academic credit.

The LEAP students, all former and current professional Bay Area dancers, are earning their bachelor of arts degrees through individualized courses of study tailored to their offstage career goals. Many complete their degrees in three to four years while dancing full-time. Already eleven San Francisco Ballet dancers, including Muriel Maffre, the first student to enroll in the program, have graduated. Some, like law student Dalene Bramer, Stephen Legate, who is in chiropractic school, and Megan Low, who is earning her master's in education, have continued into professional and graduate schools. "In the theater our bodies are working all the time," Maffre says, "so there is a need for intellectual investigation to balance the physical activity." For Smith, the benefits are more practical. "I know that eventually I'm going to stop dancing," he says, "and knowing that I will have a college degree lets me think about the future with more hope and less anxiety."

San Francisco Ballet has been supportive of the LEAP program, providing many dancers with grants to help offset the tuition. Mark Baird, a former dancer with the Joffrey Ballet and director of LEAP since 2002, remembers the 1980s when dancers were forbidden to bring even newspapers into the studios. Sheridan knows similar stories. "Muriel would meet people at parties who, when they learned she was a dancer, asked her, 'So when are you going to get a real job?' Yet traditionally in the dance world, you were suspect if you were thinking about college because it meant you weren't committed to the art form." In a small second-floor conference room at the hotel, Smith is defying both myths as he proffers an interpretation of the dancing shadows in the Allegory of the Cave. "Plato is saying that the ones who are not seeking to rule would be the best to rule," he says softly.

75 l) Damian Smith
works on a college
paper (2006)

75 r) Yuan Yuan Tan
gives a presentation
as part of the
Liberal Education
for Arts Professionals
program (2006)

76–77) A technical
rehearsal of
Helgi Tomasson's
Giselle (2005)

4

Master Class

On a rainy afternoon in late April 2003, Helgi Tomasson was standing in the center of the Christensen Studio in the San Francisco Ballet building, quietly recollecting in his body the dark and pensive male solo from George Balanchine's *Divertimento* from *Le Baiser de la Fée.* A few feet away, Gonzalo Garcia, who was then nineteen and the youngest male principal dancer in the company, studied Tomasson's actions intently. Moving just behind Tomasson, Garcia echoed the soft turns on quarter point and off-balance jumps and landings that are trademarks of this unusual moody and mysterious male solo.

"Balanchine made this entire solo on me in an hour and twenty minutes," Tomasson told Garcia. "Then he didn't rehearse me again in it until two days before the premiere. All he said was 'Good, that's good. Next!'" Tomasson recalled, laughing.

For nearly three hours, the compact and intense Garcia pushed himself, repeating again and again the startling swoops to the knees and jumps and landings that stamp this solo. The original ballet's libretto, taken from Hans Christian Andersen's *The Ice Maiden,* concerns a young man who is kissed by a fairy as a child and is revisited by her on his wedding day when she claims him as hers. Igor Stravinsky, who wrote the score, viewed this fatal kiss as an allegory about the artist who is magically imprinted with a devotion to his art. Tomasson, his hair now white, had been in New York City Ballet for barely two years, a twenty-nine-year-old virtuoso, when Balanchine created this solo on him.

78–79) Helgi Tomasson choreographs *Tuning Game* (1995)

80) Helgi Tomasson rehearses *The Dybbuk Variation* as (left to right) choreographer Jerome Robbins and composer Leonard Bernstein look on (1974)

As he danced at that moment, thirty-one years later, in front of Garcia and the camera crew who had arranged this afternoon of filming for the George Balanchine Trust, one could see past the man who is now an artistic director to the dancer he once was. As he moved, Tomasson's gestures disclosed the unaffected precision and purity of technique for which he was legendary during the fifteen years he danced with New York City Ballet and, before that, the Joffrey and Harkness Ballets. With each company, his experiences as a dancer prefigured the actions, values, and sensibility he now displays as the artistic director of San Francisco Ballet. Instead of the uncertainty and ambiguity that continued for the two years of Mrs. Harkness's sponsorship of the Joffrey Ballet, Tomasson has come to favor a candor approaching bluntness in dealing with his dancers. He uses language as economically as motion and with a reserve that colleagues like costume designer Martin Pakledinaz say make one listen to his silences. Rather than letting a star dancer siphon off all the attention and choice roles in the repertory, as Tomasson found was the situation when he initially took over San Francisco Ballet, he deliberately casts and acquires repertory to showcase as many as possible of the principal dancers and soloists, and often even corps dancers.

Tomasson also absorbed lessons about how to avoid a nationalist bias from the various strains he experienced as a young dancer. Robert Joffrey initially demanded he dance under the name *Harold* Tomasson (which he did for the touring season of 1962 until the company ended up in Seattle where Tomasson had distant relatives who helped him find other Helgis in the phone book to persuade Joffrey that his was a legitimate name for Scandinavian men). When he won the silver medal for the United States at the 1969 Moscow International Ballet Competition, the *New York Times* reporter who called to interview him ended the conversation the moment he learned Tomasson wasn't an American citizen. Today, at San Francisco Ballet, Tomasson supports a deep internationalism in both his dancers and his artistic staff. Garcia, who was born in Spain and received most of his training there, exemplifies this.

On that day in the studio, Tomasson cautioned Garcia that the dreamy look of ease in the *Baiser* steps is dangerously deceptive. "It gradually gets harder and harder," he said. "By the end you are so tired you just want to get it over with but you have to draw it out instead." In less than an hour Garcia was drenched with sweat as he learned the subtle challenges of this pensive solo. "The body is doing something and the head is doing something else," Tomasson said, marking the uncommonly beautiful motion of a series of spurting leaps in which the dancer snaps his head backward toward where he came from while his body bounds forward into the unknown.

Early Inspirations

It's tempting to read this solo as a metaphor for Helgi Tomasson's life in dance. First there is the ballet's narrative about a child's chance encounter with the demanding art around which his life will be shaped. Then there are the attributes of the solo—the balanced purity of execution, the transparent way of performing technical feats so that the dance rather than the dancer is highlighted, all qualities of Tomasson as an artist preserved by Balanchine in the solo. Finally, there is the symbolism of the choreography itself—the image of a man honoring the past while advancing into an unknown future—that marks so many of Tomasson's own transitions from a child on a tiny island in the North Atlantic Ocean to a pacesetting director of a renowned company in the world of international ballet.

Growing up as the only child of parents who divorced when he was seven years old (his half brother was born later when his mother remarried), Tomasson saw his first dance performance as a five-year-old. A touring ensemble of dancers from the Royal Danish Ballet was performing in the local theater in the little fishing village on the small Westman Islands where Tomasson and his family were living, eight miles south of the mainland of Iceland. His mother and her sister attended the dance performance and, deciding this might also be fun for young Helgi, at intermission they walked back to where they were living, two blocks away, retrieved him, and brought him with them for the second half of the show.

There the fairy kissed him. Tomasson's mother told him that from that afternoon onward whenever he heard music on the radio, he tried to imitate what he had seen onstage. Tomasson remembers this continuing for two years until his parents divorced and he and his mother moved back to Reykjavík, where he had been born. "My uncle, who was an amateur soccer player, saw me jumping around and said to my mother that she should send me to a ballet school run by his friend," Tomasson recalls. There, at the age of nine, he took his first dance class, studying ballet once or twice a week in the ballet school run by his uncle's friend, Sif Thors, and her friend, Sigridur Arman. Classes were only offered from October to early May, the Icelandic winter. "The summers are not that long," Tomasson says, noting the difficulty of having to stop dancing completely for five months every year. "So when you're a child out of school you go to work. You're either put on a farm or a fishing boat. You don't just vacation. I was lucky, I went to a farm."

By the time he was ten, Tomasson had begun studying three times a week in the winters with a Danish couple, Erik and Lisa Bidsted, who were engaged through the national theater in Iceland that had just been built. They were both teachers at the Pantomime Theatre in Copenhagen's Tivoli Gardens, and they liked Helgi, perhaps admiring his spunk—he was the only boy among two hundred girls in their school. Initially Erik Bidsted, whom Tomasson remembers as "turning and jumping a lot," told young Tomasson he wasn't any good. "I had a hard time taking dance as a child in Iceland because I was teased a lot," Tomasson says, noting that it wasn't until he turned sixteen and began studying in Copenhagen and performing at the Pantomime Theatre that he first realized he was indeed a good dancer. "But I'm stubborn. It must be an Icelandic trait. The more I was teased, the more determined I was not to give up. I think for the longest time it was a matter of pride. I had never seen boys my age dancing so it sparked competition in me. The competitiveness in me was kindled," he says. That summer, when he was ten, the Bidsteds took Tomasson with them for his first visit to Copenhagen where Erik Bidsted was a choreographer and director. Young Tomasson learned Danish very quickly and spent several weeks watching the Bidsteds work in the famed Pantomime Theatre, a nineteenth-century Danish tradition rooted in sixteenth-century commedia dell'arte stories. Tomasson's international travels had begun.

This quality of stubbornness, of not shrinking from discouragement, would be an important attribute when Tomasson assumed the leadership of San Francisco Ballet in 1985, at the height of contentious public debate over the command and direction of the company. What was stubbornness in the child became determination in the adult. "Why give up? That means you are weak," he told dance writer Selma Jeanne Cohen in an interview in 1969 about his persistence as a ballet student.

Tomasson's early experience of dance as an international passport would also inform his vision as an artistic director. The group of dancers he has assembled in San Francisco is arguably the most international in the world. It's easy to imagine it as the dream company for an itinerant dancer from a nation with no ballet tradition, who was once refused permission from studying or working at the Royal Danish Ballet in Copenhagen because he wasn't a Danish citizen. More than forty years after his arrival in the United States, Tomasson continues to have a deep affection and pride about his Icelandic origins—sentiments that signal his own internationalism and reverence for different nationalistic identities. He is esteemed as a cultural star in Iceland. In 1974 he became one of the few artists, and the youngest person ever, to receive the nation's Knight of the Order of the Falcon, and in 1990 he was awarded the Commander of the Order of the Falcon. "I'm a national hero. People know me, they followed my career," he says about the regard he has enjoyed for more than thirty years in Iceland.

The Iceland in which Tomasson grew up in the late 1940s and 1950s was a very small community—with, he estimates, a hundred thousand people in its biggest city, Reykjavík—but he remembers it as having a strong cultural life. There were two active drama theaters with opera and operetta, and he danced in some of the operettas. "People read a lot," he says. "There are marvelous writers in Iceland. Marvelous painters. For that small a country, the theater is of a very high standard."

When Tomasson was thirteen, the Bidsteds took him to spend a summer with them in Copenhagen again, and finally, on his third visit with them at the age of fifteen, Tomasson spent a summer studying at a private school, Bartholin Ballet School, in Copenhagen and performing in Tivoli Gardens with them. "At that time there were two performances a day," he recalls. "It was an outdoor theater and at 7:45 in the evening there was the first show of a half-hour of commedia dell'arte shows that rotated featuring standard figures like Harlequin. Then at 9:45 they did a half-hour ballet performance. This ran from May 1 to September 15 every day with only one holiday the whole summer. It was very good for me." There for the first time Tomasson discovered competition and determination. "I had never seen boys my age dancing before. [It was then] I decided I wanted to be a dancer," he says. In Denmark Tomasson absorbed trademarks of nineteenth-century Danish choreographer August Bournonville's training, particularly the *petit batterie* (small rapid beating steps) and the details of hand positions, qualities he would filter decades later through his teaching at San Francisco Ballet.

By the late 1950s, Tomasson was on his own, dancing regularly in Copenhagen, performing in the Pantomime Theatre in the summers, and, with a new job, dancing in the musical *My Fair Lady* in the winter. Before this new job began in October 1959, Tomasson had a couple weeks off, so he made a quick trip home to Iceland to see his mother and family. Reading a newspaper, he discovered that Jerome Robbins's small touring ensemble, Ballets: U.S.A., was performing in Reykjavík and that Robbins was with them. "I saw all the performances and I was thrilled," Tomasson said. His old local teacher, Lisa Bidsted, asked if Robbins might take Tomasson as an apprentice, but Robbins said he couldn't because he wasn't sure what was going to happen to this company. Tomasson returned to Denmark to work, and the following spring he received a letter from Robbins saying he had arranged for a scholarship for Tomasson at the School of American Ballet in New York. Tomasson regretfully deferred the scholarship to the fall, because he had already signed a contract to perform for the summer season in Copenhagen. In October 1960, two days before his eighteenth birthday, Helgi Tomasson came to the United States to study, perform, and ascend.

Helgi Tomasson in America

With the endorsement of Robbins, Tomasson studied on scholarship for several months at the School of American Ballet, taking class with former Diaghilev dancer Pierre Vladimiroff and the great Danish teacher Stanley Williams and getting by on what he called "restaurant English." Kay Mazzo, who would later dance with Tomasson at New York City Ballet, remembers the immediate buzz created by Robbins's discovery of Tomasson. "I first heard about Helgi in 1961. I was dancing with Jerome Robbins's Ballets: U.S.A. in Europe, and we all heard about this wonderful young dancer that Jerry had seen. The next thing I heard was Helgi was being sent to our ballet school—the School of American Ballet—Jerry felt that was the place Helgi should study," Mazzo recalls. "Even as a young dancer Helgi was a superb technician. He had an artistry that was very special and a sincerity in his dancing that was very much his own."

After seven months of study, however, Tomasson's money ran out and he returned to Denmark where he met the great Danish dancer, Erik Bruhn, who wrote letters of introduction for him to Robert Joffrey and to American Ballet Theatre. Tomasson saved up his money again and returned to New York in October 1961 to audition for Joffrey. However, Joffrey toyed with Tomasson, playing hard to get after Tomasson auditioned and not letting him know whether or not he had been taken into the company until his money ran out two months later. At that point, according to Joffrey's biographer Sasha Anawalt, Joffrey offered Tomasson a loan, telling him he would not be paid for rehearsals and could join the company only if he changed his name to Harold. Reluctantly, Tomasson agreed.

83

84) Helgi Tomasson,
age ten, at the
National Theatre
of Iceland (1952)

85 t) Helgi Tomasson
in George Balanchine's
Vienna Waltzes (1978)

85 b) Lew Christensen
rehearses *Norwegian Moods*
with Helgi Tomasson
in the New York
State Theater (1982)

Tomasson performed with the Joffrey for two years, dancing in a broad repertory of contemporary works and touring internationally with the company, but also experiencing firsthand the tensions between a willful patroness, Mrs. Harkness, and a passionate director, Joffrey. One day, six months after he joined the Joffrey, Tomasson noticed a pretty young woman sitting in the lobby of the Joffrey studio, having just finished auditioning for the company. She was Marlene Rizzo, an American dancer of Italian descent. Tomasson was immediately attracted to her. The next day he summoned the courage to ask her out for coffee.

Tomasson and Rizzo danced together in several works in the Joffrey repertory, and when the company disbanded in 1964 they both were taken into the new company, the Harkness Ballet, which Mrs. Harkness formed in its place. Prior to the company's first European tour, Tomasson married Rizzo in Reykjavík on December 26, 1964. They started their family soon afterward; Kristinn was born in 1967, and their second son, Erik, in 1971. "It must have been hard for Helgi," commented Patricia McBride, his frequent dancing partner at New York City Ballet, about the rarity of being a professional dancer and a parent in the company in the 1970s. "He was always a family man. He would just go home to his family after performances."

Marlene stopped dancing in 1970 to care for the family. "It's a high and no dancer ever gets over it," she said of her years of performing. "But I think it's made it easier for Helgi that I've been there to understand his problems. Very few dancers manage to have a solid family relationship. Dancing is always an 'I,' and a family is definitely a 'we,'" she told critic Allan Ulrich in a 1985 interview from the Tomassons' home in New Jersey just prior to their move to San Francisco. "Your feet are planted firmly on the ground as a parent," Tomasson once observed about being a dancer and a father. "You are involved with what your children are doing at school. It's not ballet all the time."

Yet it does seem to be ballet *much* of the time. Marlene has been a warm, gentle, unofficial but steady presence by Tomasson's side for most of his professional career and certainly during his tenure at San Francisco Ballet. "She knows me so well," he has explained about his wife. "She knows what I would like to achieve and do." While neither of the Tomasson sons danced, the youngest one, Erik, who trained as a cinematographer, became the official photographer for San Francisco Ballet in 2005.

Perhaps because he married at twenty-three and became a father at twenty-five, Tomasson has been, by several accounts, very accommodating to the unusually large number of dancers in his company who are parents, or about to become parents. Former San Francisco Ballet soloist Sherri LeBlanc remembers with amusement an exchange she had with Tomasson when he continued to cast her in ballets months after she became pregnant. "For as long as he could, he'd get me onstage. He let me go out there onstage in a pastel leotard in *Dreams of Harmony* when I was about three months pregnant," she says. Afterward when she asked him how she looked, he smiled, "You look healthy!"

Compassion for the full life of a dancer off the stage as well as on is one of the personal attributes of Tomasson as a director that his dancers and staff mention most frequently. Ashley Wheater had been a principal dancer with San Francisco Ballet from 1989 to 1996 when a serious neck injury ended his dancing career. He vividly recalls Tomasson visiting him in the hospital as he underwent repeated surgeries and assuring him that, whatever happened, there would be a place for him working with the company. "I remember being stuck at home in a brace from my neck to my hips afterward and unable to imagine even working again. Helgi persuaded me to come back to the studio to begin rehearsing two principal dancers for *Swan Lake* in 1996 and it was just what I needed," says Wheater, who became ballet master that year and assistant to the artistic director in 2002, functioning as a key part of the company's artistic staff. "He is an exceptional man. There are very few people that I would say really have integrity, and I think it applies to Helgi. He is a really decent human being. As long as he is here I want to be here."

One of the features that is an essential part of Tomasson's elevation of San Francisco Ballet into a company of world stature has been the creation of an active international touring program. This, too, has roots in Tomasson's own past as a dancer—during the seven years he danced with Joffrey and Harkness, the companies toured incessantly, and he experienced firsthand the validation that comes from global exposure and acclaim. In 1964, his first year with the Harkness Ballet, Tomasson was named a principal dancer while the company was on tour in Portugal. Throughout the European tours he had been very successful dancing modern works by contemporary American choreographers including George Skibine, Brian MacDonald, and Stuart Hodes. Then in 1969 the Harkness company manager approached Tomasson and said that Mrs. Harkness would like to send him to Moscow to compete in the first International Ballet Competition. Harkness suggested he might be interested in seeing other dancers, and Tomasson agreed, on the condition that Marlene accompany him.

86–87) Helgi Tomasson rehearses *Swan Lake* with Lorena Feijoo (2006)

89) Helgi Tomasson directs Sarah Van Patten and Pierre-François Vilanoba at a technical rehearsal of Tomasson's *Romeo and Juliet* (2005)

It turned out to be an extraordinary experience for Tomasson, who arrived with his wife and his music, and little else. The other competitors from around the world—nearly eighty—traveled with support staffs of accompanists, teachers, and coaches. The competition wore on for several days as contestants were regularly eliminated and Tomasson steadily advanced. Lacking anyone other than himself and Marlene to stand in line and lobby for rehearsal space, accompanists, and lighting rehearsals, Tomasson kept progressing through the taxing rounds of competitive dancing. Only when it was announced that he was a finalist did he realize the instructions he had read were confusing and he needed a sixth solo, and a costume, immediately. Talking with Marlene and some Danish dancers who were also competing, Tomasson decided to perform the male variation from the *Black Swan Pas de Deux* from *Swan Lake*—which he had never danced and which he had only a day and a half to prepare. By now the precise, dark-haired, slender, five-foot seven-inch dancer from the United States had become an audience favorite. Even the judges responded, and when the great ballerina Galina Ulanova, the head of the jury of twenty judges, learned that Tomasson needed a costume for the *Black Swan*, she gave him special permission to look through the Bolshoi Ballet's wardrobes to find something that fit.

"In Moscow they like spectacular dancers but they want something else, too," Tomasson said afterward. "I am not a flashy dancer; I am more of a lyrical dancer and they liked what I did. There were lots of dancers at the competition who could jump higher than I did and turn more than I did. But here was something I did that the audience liked, and the judges, too," he recalled. Most remarkably, the tenser it got, the more assured it seemed Tomasson's performing became. An archival film fragment of the competition remains, and in it Tomasson executes a series of perfect entrechat sixes, looking both happy and comfortable in the midst of a series of clenched muscle performances by the anxious male soloists before and after him. "It takes a lot to throw him onstage," Marlene says of Tomasson. "He has all his nerves before, but the minute he passes through that stage door they disappear."

Early the following morning Tomasson received a call from his interpreter—he had won the silver medal. Mikhail Baryshnikov, then a star with the Kirov Ballet Company, won the gold. "It was a turning point in my career," Tomasson told dance writer Eric Taub in 1979. "I won a silver medal dancing classical solos, and what am I doing at home? Rolling around on the floor wearing kneepads. No, that's not for me. It was time to move on."

Although the mainstream American press essentially ignored Tomasson's prize because his citizenship was Icelandic rather than American, the dance world took note. Even before the Moscow competition, Tomasson had decided he was ready to leave Harkness, which folded during its final European tour. "So I came to New York and spoke to Mr. Balanchine and a few weeks later I was in [New York City Ballet]," he said simply, not mentioning the several offers he had received from European companies.

The years Tomasson spent with New York City Ballet gave him a repertory that highlighted his extraordinary musicality and lyrical phrasing and satisfied his appetite for performing in the neoclassical idiom. In many ways these were the late glory years of Balanchine—the period in which he choreographed his final round of masterpieces before his death in 1983. Within Tomasson's first few years at New York City Ballet, both Balanchine and Robbins made major roles for him. These included the male solo in Balanchine's 1972 *Divertimento* from *Le Baiser de la Fée* and his *Symphony in Three Movements.* Robbins featured him in *Goldberg Variations,* which demanded of Tomasson playful rhythms deployed against the high virtuosity of multiple pirouettes and fouetté turns. Another side of him was revealed in Robbins's 1974 *The Dybbuk Variations,* where Tomasson infused mystical drama into the passionate runs, flying lifts, and jagged jumps of the lead male role. Tomasson's summers of apprenticeship in the pantomime theater had honed his mime skills, and these were highlighted at New York City Ballet when in 1974, in pointed tribute to his presence in the company, according to Lincoln Kirstein, Balanchine worked with Alexandra Danilova to present a revival of *Coppélia* with Patricia McBride and Tomasson heading the cast of this comic romantic ballet.

By the mid-1970s the American dance press had taken note, and Tomasson was profiled in cover stories and features in *Dance Magazine, Ballet News,* and the *Boston Globe.* In 1979 *New York Times* dance critic Anna Kisselgoff wrote about Tomasson in a string of superlatives: "Purity, elegance, verve, clarity, precision and perfection." For a Sunday feature on him, she wrote as her opening sentences: "These are the words to which one has consistently returned when writing about Helgi Tomasson's dancing for more than a decade. He is quite simply one of the few male classical dancers in ballet who could be termed truly great." Kisselgoff expanded on this several years later in summing up Tomasson's career on the occasion of his retirement in January 1985. "He knew how to filter the emotional through a crystal-clear classical prism," she wrote. "As the model of a Balanchine dancer, he enabled Balanchine, who had never before had dancers of Mr. Tomasson's caliber, to show off his own choreography for men at its most classical."

In the final years of Tomasson's dancing career, the ballet world underwent a seismic shift as the founding directors of the leading dance companies began to pass away. In October 1984, eighteen months after Balanchine succumbed, San Francisco Ballet's guiding force, Lew Christensen, died. The morning that Christensen passed away of a massive heart attack, Tomasson was returning to New York after meetings with the Royal Danish Ballet in Copenhagen about the possibility of taking over as artistic director. Within a few days he was on a plane headed back to San Francisco, having been asked by Lincoln Kirstein to represent him at Christensen's memorial service. "Knowing Lincoln, he had another motive in sending me there," Tomasson told interviewer Cheryl Ossola with a smile.

DANCING WITH
HELGI

A test of a great male dancer is his partnering ability, and the best person to comment on that skill is the ballerina. For the fifteen years he danced with New York City Ballet, Helgi Tomasson's most constant partner was the petite and supple Patricia McBride. "He was a wonderful partner," says McBride. "Helgi knew me so well I could just throw myself and he'd be there," she says, referring to his ability to catch her and keep her balanced.

In July 1971, the first summer Tomasson was in the company, he and his wife and young son shared a house with McBride and her husband, fellow New York City Ballet dancer Jean-Pierre Bonnefoux, in Saratoga for the month of July. "Helgi was learning the repertory," McBride recalls. "He and Jean-Pierre always shared a dressing room. It was a very nice atmosphere—a friendly, wonderful, warm feeling from the start. Because of our physicality, we were partners. So we had a good time, and we worked hard."

That first year Jerome Robbins cast Tomasson in the intricate and complicated *Goldberg Variations,* where he reserved the slowest, most thoughtful and directly emotional duet for McBride and Tomasson. "We got to know one another through *Goldberg Variations.* It was such a long process," she says. "But Helgi was a natural partner." Robbins followed this with his 1974 *The Dybbuk Variations* where he created the central couple of Chanon and Leah on Tomasson and McBride. In this ballet they move from a love duet of passionate runs and flying lifts to a fiercely locked, twisting duet, as Chanon's dead spirit possesses Leah. A critic once commented about the subtle intelligence of their perfectly matched emotionalism: "McBride and Tomasson demonstrate how well they understood that silver core of stillness that runs through much of Robbins's choreography." The two were also an indelible partnership in George Balanchine's *Divertimento* from *Le Baiser de la Fée* and his restaging of *Coppélia.*

"Helgi was such a pure classical dancer. Clean, beautiful, strong technique," McBride says. "Dancing with Helgi, I discovered how it takes two to make one performance."

91) Alexandra Danilova
rehearses George Balanchine/
Alexandra Danilova's
Coppélia with Patricia McBride
and Helgi Tomasson
(1974)

91

94

92) Sabina Allemann
and Ashley Wheater
in Helgi Tomasson's
Valses Poeticos (1990)

93) Vanessa Zahorian
and Nicolas Blanc
in Helgi Tomasson's
Blue Rose (2006)

94) Parrish Maynard
in Helgi Tomasson's
Chi-Lin (2002)

95) Hansuke Yamamoto
in Helgi Tomasson's
Concerto Grosso (2006)

LEAD AND FOLLOW:
TRAINING FOR ARTISTIC LEADERSHIP

Questioned if he sees himself as a mentor, Helgi Tomasson winces. "Does that mean I'm getting older?" he asks with a smile. Wisdom, success, and, yes, age, mark his reign as the artistic director of San Francisco Ballet. Already two of Tomasson's former dancers are leading major ballet companies—Mikko Nissinen took over Boston Ballet in 2001 and Christopher Stowell was named artistic director of Oregon Ballet Theatre in 2003—and both cite having watched Tomasson repair and rebuild San Francisco Ballet from within as pivotal in shaping their own styles of artistic leadership.

"I was very fortunate that at the time I joined San Francisco Ballet Helgi was in an early stage of putting his ship together," says Nissinen, who danced with the company from 1987 to 1996. "Helgi made good choices. He hired people who were technically good and serious about the profession. He was able to see what sort of person everybody was and we were busy dancing all the time." "Busy dancers equal happy dancers" is consequently item one on Nissinen's how-to list for making a company.

Nissinen knew from the time he was eighteen that he wanted to direct his own company, and he studied Tomasson closely. "Helgi's way of nurturing dancers is exposing them to a repertory and training," Nissinen says. "He wants good-quality dance with musicality and simple presentation that doesn't distract from the big goal of the piece, which is to dance with integrity, taste, and quality."

Tomasson has set works for Nissinen's and Stowell's companies, inaugurating their new relationship as director colleagues. They cite enviously Tomasson's frequent international travels in search of new choreographers and dancers, but, Stowell sighs, in order to copy *that,* he'll need a bigger budget.

"Understatement, musicality, and Mark Morris" are three key Tomasson values that Nissinen emulates. Mark Morris? "Helgi has been very, very smart in bringing Mark in," Nissinen says. "He helped San Francisco Ballet tremendously because after doing his works the company danced Balanchine better, they danced Tomasson better. When I started running my company, the first thing, I picked up the phone and told Mark, 'I'd love to have a work of yours.'"

Helgi Tomasson Comes to San Francisco

In the New York State Theatre on Sunday, January 27, 1985, the night of Tomasson's farewell performance, were two emissaries from the San Francisco Ballet board of trustees—search committee chairman Thomas J. Perkins and committee member L. Jay Tenenbaum. Shortly before this farewell performance, Tomasson had called Perkins and said that if he'd like to see him dance he should come to New York the following week, without saying it would be his final performance. "The audience knew Helgi was retiring, and following his performance the audience stood for twenty solid minutes in a standing ovation," Tenenbaum recalls. "They wouldn't sit down. It was stirring to see and it made us feel 'Boy, we got the right guy!'" While New York was saying good-bye to Tomasson in the ovation that followed the final curtain as he disappeared backward into the wings in the *Divertimento* from *Le Basier de la Fée*, San Francisco was saying hello.

On July 1, 1985, Tomasson began his directorship of San Francisco Ballet with a three-year contract, capping months of an international search by the company for a new director and the screening of more than seventy-five candidates. In February Tomasson and his family had come to San Francisco to meet the mayor and press. "I'm hopeful that the conflicts that have plagued the ballet these last five months are over," Mayor Dianne Feinstein said in her greeting to Tomasson, referring to the acrimonious firing and then rehiring of the company's co-director, Michael Smuin, the previous fall.

One of the first things Tomasson did was to reassure the dancers that the rumors circulating about everyone getting fired were just that—rumors. "What sparked my interest in coming here were the dancers," he said. "They are wonderful material. I want to take this company on to the next plateau," he continued. "There is only one ballet company in this city so its repertory has to be wide ranging. This is a classically oriented company and we will work in a classical idiom." In one broad stroke he had mapped the future of the company.

Among those in the audience at Tomasson's farewell performance in New York was an eighteen-year-old School of American Ballet student, Christopher Stowell. He contacted Tomasson about a job, and within a week he had been hired as a member of the corps, dancing in works by both Tomasson and Smuin, who remained as a choreographer for a final year. Stowell describes what the transition of Tomasson's arrival felt like from the inside—as an inversion of the standards Smuin had worked with where personalities were more the focus and roles were created around them. "But suddenly those roles weren't there anymore and people were getting really exposed and some people didn't look good at all in the new repertoire," Stowell says. He notes that Tomasson started building for strength on the stage in the classroom by making what turned out to be a controversial request that the women wear pointe shoes in company class.

After two seasons Tomasson instituted a ranking system identifying each dancer as corps de ballet, soloist, or principal dancer, which irritated some of the older dancers even more. "I remember thinking he was very generous about it in most cases," Stowell continues. "He respected people's pasts. But it was also a polite way of saying, 'You should probably not be here anymore.'"

Val Caniparoli, a character dancer and choreographer with the company who was dancing when Tomasson became director, remembers the first year of transition as "creepy." "It was not a healthy environment," he says. "You could tell it was difficult when Helgi took over because he was still analyzing dancers and repertory and still having to deal with the controversy. But the longer he stayed, the more the problems diminished."

Anita Paciotti, a character dancer and ballet mistress with San Francisco Ballet, was still dancing principal roles with the company when Tomasson arrived, and she remembers the abrupt turnaround it prompted with her own career. "I had been dancing for eighteen years when Helgi became artistic director. I was thirty-six, and I couldn't possibly have joined the company at that age. The women started wearing pointe shoes in class!" says Paciotti, who retired within Tomasson's first year. "Things were very different and he wanted to establish his own dancers right away—he had to make space." By the end of his first two years as San Francisco Ballet's new artistic director, Tomasson had made more than space. He had turned around the artistic fortunes of the company, and the years of accumulated deficits were rapidly shrinking. As he stripped away the last vestiges of San Francisco Ballet's regionalism, he propelled it into position as a major international dance power. The nation's leading dance writers praised the dramatically visible changes Tomasson had orchestrated in such a remarkably short time. He was moving the company back to the basics of classicism, back to virtuosity without glitz. And he was doing it by deeds rather than words. On Tomasson's tenth anniversary with the company he told a critic simply, "San Francisco Ballet reflects who I am."

101) Helgi Tomasson
working in the studio
(2006)

William Forsythe Stages *Artifact Suite*

"This is the center of the new dance universe," Patrick Corbin said softly as he gazed across the studio at the more than seventy dancers of San Francisco Ballet listening attentively to choreographer William Forsythe. Forsythe, who had arrived the night before from Japan, was visiting on a two-day blitz to prepare the company for the American premiere of his *Artifact Suite* in April of 2006, before continuing on to his own company in Frankfurt, Germany. Corbin sat against the wall of mirrors at the one end of the company's big fourth-floor Christensen Studio along with a small private audience of ballet staff, donors, and select friends who were being allowed to observe this customarily most hidden of dance processes: how a ballet company acquires its repertory.

Just a few days earlier, Corbin, a former leading dancer with the Paul Taylor Dance Company, had been the featured guest adding to the San Francisco Ballet repertory in this studio, as he refreshed the dancers' physical memory of *Spring Rounds.* The company had premiered *Spring Rounds,* Taylor's blithe dance of youthful passions, on tour in Paris the previous summer, the third Taylor work in the repertory. "They were absolutely gorgeous. It was really very cool," Corbin said of his several weeks' experience first of teaching, and then of rehearsing, the dancers in Taylor's modern dance piece. "They dance with their entire bodies. And they're not cookie-cutter bodies. Helgi has different body types and different dancing types and that's making a beautiful mix. They're also *beautiful* to look at, every single one of them," New York–based Corbin sighed, gesturing toward the dancers.

Artifact Suite and *Spring Rounds* are two of the twenty-two ballets that San Francisco Ballet dances on average every season, which also includes the three to six new works that are commissioned each year. All are part of the five hundred dances whose costumes sit in plastic containers in the ballet's warehouse with the potential of someday being revived. Each of these ballets is chosen, commissioned, or—in the instance of one or two dances each year—created by Tomasson himself, as a way to showcase and extend the depth of dancing talent in the company. Repertory choices are always measured against aesthetic and budget constraints as Tomasson travels internationally in search of ballets to round out the diversity of each of the eight annual programs, balance the physical demands on the dancers, and keep them and the audiences excited about "the rep."

"Helgi has collected such an extraordinary diversity of really exceptional artists in this company," Ashley Wheater, ballet master, says. "He's taken them and challenged them and rewarded them. Because the reward is getting these incredible works to dance." Mark Morris, who has more of his works in the San Francisco Ballet repertory than any company outside his own, agrees that Tomasson is a fine curator of repertory as well as dancers. "Most companies do the same old tired bull— all the time," Morris says. "Everybody buys the same model choreography from somebody. Helgi doesn't, he's more of a connoisseur. You know there aren't many companies that are this good." Pascal Molat, who danced with several companies in Europe prior to coming to San Francisco Ballet, says that from the dancer's standpoint it was the diversity of the repertory that attracted him. "I saw the company doing a piece of Balanchine, a piece of Mark Morris— it was very eclectic," Molat says of a visit he made from France. "I thought, that's great! A little bit of history, a little bit of fun."

For guest choreographers like Morris, Forsythe, Lar Lubovitch, and Christopher Wheeldon, the reward of having one of their dances taken into the San Francisco Ballet repertory is the gift of freedom of invention and time with the company. "Helgi requests a new work and then he respectfully gets out of the way," says Lar Lubovitch, who eschews the label "modern dance" for *Elemental Brubeck*, the jazzy film noir–inspired dance he created for the company's 2005 Paris season. "Helgi just opens the door to his company to a visiting choreographer without imposing rules or judgments. It's a very privileged place to work, with the ballet building, opera house, technical support, and orchestra," he says a bit enviously.

Wheeldon, who has created four works for the company, agrees. "Helgi has assembled a group of dancers that really understands the process of making new work. For me that process is partly collaborative," Wheeldon says. "I like to work with dancers who are excited about giving their input as artists in the studio, and these dancers are very creative and incredibly talented." Tomasson has said that in his early years directing San Francisco Ballet he could call a choreographer on the phone and ask him for a work for the company, and he would say yes, knowing Tomasson's reputation as a dancer. Beginning in the early 1990s, the reputation of what he was accomplishing as an artistic director rivaled his legacy as a dancer, and the roster of choreographers eager to work with the company grew.

With few exceptions, every work Tomasson has acquired revolves around the consistent core of San Francisco Ballet—rigorous classical ballet—so it provides a commentary on, challenge to, or development of the classical ballet lexicon. More than one colleague has observed that the Tomasson-era San Francisco Ballet seems to be combining the best of what he found at Joffrey, Harkness, and New York City Ballets and centered on his own appetite as a dancer for a diverse but classical repertory to dance. When Tomasson commissioned *New Sleep* in 1987, San Francisco Ballet's first work from Forsythe, reportedly at the suggestion of Ballet Mistress Bonita Borne, many in American dance regarded Forsythe as a risky expatriate renegade. Their opinion was seemingly confirmed with *New Sleep*, with its ear-splitting electronic score by Tom Willems, oddly aggressive partnering, and use of the wings rather than the audience as the facing toward which much of the dance seemed to be directed. When *Artifact Suite*, the fourth Forsythe ballet acquired by San Francisco Ballet, received its American premiere during the company's 2006 home season, it played to standing-room audiences, and *San Francisco Chronicle* critic Rachel Howard applauded its "postmodern brilliance" as an "of-this-age envelope pushing" spectacle. Tomasson was building an enlightened ballet public through ballets consciously acquired not to give audiences what they want so much as to motivate them to value and understand the elegance of what they get.

In the fourth-floor studio prior to the company premiere, Forsythe was working intently with four couples at the front of the room while the rest of the company looked on. "You have to want it more than she does," Forsythe said to Damian Smith and his partner Yuan Yuan Tan, pushing Smith to break the standard man-showing-off-the-woman partnering mold by being as showy, active, and physically extended in the pas de deux as the woman. Smith's quietly elegant manner became fiercer as he grasped and stretched Tan's extended arms by the wrists, twisting away from her at the same time. "You have to be the other half, use your heads," Forsythe coached, pushing the dancers to elongate their necks in opposition to their twisting bodies as he circled close to Smith and Tan. Jodie Gates, Forsythe's rehearsal assistant who had worked with the dancers months earlier when she initially set the choreography, stood to one side of Forsythe, silently gesturing to Tan how to reach her long arms farther behind herself as she arced her head away from Smith in response to Forsythe's directive. It was a startling image of closeness serrated by opposition—classic partnering stripped down to a raw trust between two cantilevered bodies.

Ricardo Bustamante flanked Forsythe on the other side, intently copying the actions of both Tan and Smith as if imprinting them on his body. A video camera was running behind him, but as San Francisco Ballet's ballet master entrusted with learning and remembering this ballet for the future, Bustamante was the most critical recording device in the room. He was how this piece of repertory was being saved and will later be rehearsed, recalled, and preserved. Watching a master at work as his dance enters the repertory can also function as a choreographic tutorial, revealing a lot about how a dance is put together. Yuri Possokhov, who was about to retire at the end of the season after twelve years as a principal dancer and transition into a choreographer in residence for San Francisco Ballet, watched intently, half hidden under a portable barre at the side of the room.

Usually when a work is being set on the company, all three or four casts of principals who might perform it rehearse at the same time, soaking up as much of the choreographer's instruction as possible. Soloist Frances Chung, a winning, small, quick soubrette, was also learning the lead female role on the off chance a fifth woman would be needed as a backup. She stood at the very back of the studio dancing everything the front couples were with her phantom partner. The effect was like watching a time-lapsed image of the season to come, a replay of highlights that haven't yet happened, deployed simultaneously. The other pairs of principal couples were scattered a few feet away from Smith and Tan, and they followed every correction Forsythe gave. Off to another side, the regal and beautifully placed Muriel Maffre tangled with the attentive and sensuous Pierre-François Vilanoba as they worked to find the movements and the push-pull dynamic of their duet.

Next Forsythe turned his attention to the women in the corps. "Show me everything you know about the *port de bras*," he said. The luxuriously sensual Lily Rogers, Brooke Taylor Moore, Hayley Farr, Courtney Elizabeth, and Pauli Magierek each sprang onto their pointes on one leg, their other leg bent and held tucked high into the standing thigh in *passé*. In unison the women pressed their arms outward past the formal positions of the classic ballet carriage of the arms, into extravagantly overextended postures echoing the wings of a massive bird. "You are the experts here in the room. Show me," Forsythe said. "*Epaulement* is a conversation between your foot and hands. So make a wonderful conversation."

As he demonstrated, Forsythe kept discarding and tweaking movements in his ballet like a master potter at the wheel, rejecting pots that look finished and perfectly formed to everyone else. Throughout the afternoon the dancers remained sharply attentive, absorbing Forsythe's comments and giving back their understanding in speedily modified body positions and a sharpened edge of attack. Sometimes Forsythe demonstrated as he talked, moving quickly and fluidly and with a seemingly sticky consistency to his actions. Three student dancers standing by the doorway commented appreciatively on how well the fifty-six-year-old Forsythe moved for a big man. "You have to check your fear at the door," one whispered to the other, acknowledging the air of physical risk in the room.

Under Forsythe's direction, the rehearsal process was becoming an interrogation of core movements of the ballet vocabulary. "Your *rond de jambe* should be like I had a rock on the end of a string and you throw it!" he explained at one point. "Surprise me!" he requested at another. "I don't want to know what's coming." Working as swiftly as a modern dance choreographer inventing steps as he went, Forsythe was trying to wrest from San Francisco Ballet dancers the logic, the momentum, the *physics* of a ballet movement phrase, without the expected look. "Deepen your understanding of what an arabesque is," he instructed the impassioned and pliant Lorena Feijoo and her partner, the marvelously plastic Pascal Molat. "Pascal Molat is the hungriest, most genuinely curious dancer I've seen in a long time," Corbin observed quietly. "And *gorgeous*. He is so invested in the process. He's always asking, 'What if?'"

Far more than the memorization of steps was going on in this room. There was absorption of the choreographer's intent, the ambition that underlies the movements he was conveying. The clarity and strength of San Francisco Ballet dancers' training equip them to thrive in this climate of aesthetic cross training. They perform choreography from Paul Taylor to William Forsythe to Mark Morris to Jerome Robbins and Agnes de Mille, quickly adapting to the specific quality of each work. "The time is gone when you danced only the classic ballets like the Russian classic, or when I was with New York City Ballet it was either Balanchine or Robbins," Tomasson explains. "Today dancers need to be able to dance everything. You have to be a versatile dancer. I have always stressed that with the company. You have to really work at it to find what the choreographer wants stylistically, so you can change keys fast," he says. "I think that's one of the more fun challenges of dancing, because it also keeps up your own interest as a dancer."

108) Yuan Yuan Tan in Mark Morris's *Sylvia* (2006)

109) Mark Morris in the studio (2004)

110) Christopher Wheeldon
rehearses *Quaternary* ©
(2005)

111) David Arce and
Rachel Viselli in
Christopher Wheeldon's
Continuum © (2006)

112) Muriel Maffre and
Pierre-François Vilanoba
in William Forsythe's
Artifact Suite (2006)

113) William Forsythe
rehearses *Artifact Suite*
with Lorena Feijoo and
Pascal Molat (2006)

MARK MORRIS
ON HELGI TOMASSON

One of the things Mark Morris enjoys most about being a guest choreographer at San Francisco Ballet is that Artistic Director Helgi Tomasson doesn't watch. He watches the finished performances of Morris's ballets, certainly, but only after granting Morris complete freedom to cast, teach, rehearse, and costume the ballets he creates. Morris finds this freedom remarkable in the closely controlled world of professional ballet.

This faith typifies the signature Tomasson has put on San Francisco Ballet as a company that celebrates the uniqueness of the individual voice, what Morris, who has created six ballets for the company, affectionately calls "weirdness." "Helgi has very good and curious taste in choreography and dancers," Morris says. "These are great dancers. People want to come work here. And that's only become more so over the years. *Curious taste* meaning the dancers are very distinct and interesting. San Francisco Ballet is a company of human beings, instead of dead people or some crazy pink clones."

The repertory that Tomasson has assembled is as varied and distinct as his dancers. He consistently fits one to the other, using his own sophisticated and complex ballets and careful commissioning of other dances to refine and challenge the dancers. "Helgi does something artistic directors never have the sense to do," says Morris. "He hires very good choreographers and wonderful dancers and supplies them with work custom-made."

Artistically as well as administratively, Morris sees Tomasson as breaking the mold that defines most ballet company directors. "Helgi is a connoisseur, a curator. He's also a far better choreographer than most people who run companies," Morris says, noting the ambitiousness of his dances. "The dances he makes up are very, very difficult and very challenging to the dancers. I really like them. I like that approach."

All of these achievements, Morris notes, are doubly remarkable because they have unfolded in a city without another major ballet company to spur San Francisco Ballet competitively forward. "San Francisco Ballet is the only ballet company in San Francisco, and this could make it smug," Morris says. "Instead the company is as good as anything else in the world."

114) George Balanchine's
The Four Temperaments
(2005)

115) Helgi Tomasson
and Mark Morris at the
Stern Grove Festival
(circa 1995)

Life Inside the Repertory

Each season the dancers' bodies contain an astounding density of movement narratives, and the skill of this layering comes home with particular immediacy when dress rehearsals begin on the Opera House stage just prior to opening nights. There the dancers can often be glimpsed practicing one ballet while in costume for another. As if someone were flipping a switch, suddenly the *Spring Rounds* men in their vivid green poly-chiffon shirts and chartreuse tights might pivot, turn in unison, and rest their elbows on their upraised knees in the cowboys-on-horseback image from the opening of *Rodeo*. Farther upstage one of the cowboys practices his weighted lunging runs from *Spring Rounds* as *Rodeo*'s Cowgirl and the Head Wrangler work with Christine Sarry on the timing of his slow-motion walk in the one example onstage at this instant where costume and choreography match.

"If you don't maintain your roles and rehearse them up until the moment you go onstage, they're not going to be there," explains Muriel Maffre. During the season every available studio and working hour of the dancers' lives serves the repertory. "We're using our bodies—nothing stays. It's impermanent," she says, pinpointing a central paradox of the force of the dancing figure that works so hard to make a statement written on air.

As ephemeral as those moments of glory onstage are, they are noted and rewarded. Everything in a ballet company's life organizes around the repertory. Tomasson often uses the occasion of a particularly wonderful performance by a dancer to greet him or her backstage with the surprise announcement of a promotion. After Rory Hohenstein dazzled with explosive power in the fleet solo in *Elemental Brubeck*, Tomasson congratulated him backstage by telling him he had just been named a soloist. Garrett Anderson, a bright, muscular dancer, had received word about his promotion to soloist a few days earlier after his extraordinary dancing in Possokhov's grand *Reflections*.

Tomasson's own history as a dancer at times announces itself in surprising ways through the repertory. In May 1995 Tomasson presented San Francisco's first international ballet festival in the Opera House, UNited We Dance. Inviting thirteen companies from five continents to showcase their work and dancers in a six-day festival, the huge event announced San Francisco Ballet's arrival on the international dance scene as a host and artistic force. As critic Clive Barnes wrote about the festival in *Dance Magazine*, "If Tomasson had planned his San Francisco adventure to demonstrate that his own company was now indeed a world-class troupe comfortably capable of holding its own amid any international hierarchy, he could hardly have planned it better." In preparing for the 2005–06 season's evening of dances by Jerome Robbins, Tomasson joined Robbins Rights Trust representative Jean Pierre Frohlich in giving corrections to the dancers performing the choreographer's *Afternoon of a Faun* and *Dybbuk*, ballets that Tomasson danced to great acclaim with New York City Ballet. As Tomasson gave the dancers in *Faun* a few corrections afterward, his body sympathetically echoed the choreographic moment he was describing to Moises Martin where he barely peeked out from behind his partner, Patricia McBride, to see himself in the ballet's imaginary mirror. Then he gestured to Yuan Yuan Tan how McBride would reach back to tie an imaginary loose ribbon on her toe shoe without ever turning her head. Once repertory enters a dancer's body, it never completely leaves.

The repertory is also how San Francisco Ballet has created its identity, and full-length ballets have been a particularly important part of the company's history. Three years after he became artistic director, Tomasson inaugurated the company's return to classicism with his critically acclaimed 1988 production of *Swan Lake* featuring costumes and scenery by Jens-Jacob Worsaae and assistance in staging the second act by Irina Jacobson. In a production that was fresh and deeply classical, Tomasson staked out the future of the company and effectively repudiated the weakest parts of its past.

At an international conference of dance critics held in San Francisco the weekend of *Swan Lake*'s opening, Tomasson spoke about the dual interests of his affection for Tchaikovsky's score and his desire to create a production with more consistent narrative logic. "First and foremost my inspiration was really the music," he said. "I find it glorious and irresistible. It has to be danced to. Of course, I had seen the ballet dozens of times on many, many different companies—and I've always loved the ballet. But I felt that having seen the ballet so often I finally wanted to put it together the way I felt it should be. Particularly with the fourth act I felt the story should continue right out of the third act."

America's First *Swan Lake*

Tomasson had intuitively tapped into a distinguished piece of San Francisco Ballet's repertory history with his staging of *Swan Lake*. In 1940, just two years into *his* tenure as director of San Francisco Ballet, Willam Christensen had mounted the first four-act production of *Swan Lake* ever staged in the United States. Christensen's impulse had been twofold: he wanted to Americanize classical dance and he wanted to put San Francisco Ballet, along with his choreographic talents, on the national dance map as formidable artistic forces in the western United States. For Christensen, lack of knowledge was no impediment: "Like many other Americans at that time, I was simply not familiar with the full-length version," he said. "I was attracted by the score: It's great, dramatic music—music that has the drama built right into it. Finally I decided I had the nerve to tackle it."

Christensen then proceeded to "pick everyone's brains" in an effort to put together what would prove to be a landmark production for the company and the nation. He turned to San Francisco's large colony of Russian émigrés to sort through the choreography and staging. Seemingly without irony, Christensen dedicated the production to "the preservation of Russian culture in San Francisco," a pragmatic gesture that aligned him with the interests of the Tchaikovsky Centennial Committee, headed by the Prince and Princess Vasili Romanoff of San Francisco, who generously funded his production. Two ballerinas, Janet Reed and Jacqueline Martin, split the role of Odette/Odile, for the practical reason, it was reported, that neither felt sufficiently strong enough to get through the whole ballet by herself. The local and national press was chauvinistically ecstatic about the production. Richard Hays, critic for the *Seattle Times,* began his review with the following warning: "Russia must look to its ballet or America will take it away and so completely that only tradition will remain."

Christensen may have had some sense of the enormity of his undertaking, but most of his small company of twenty dancers did not. Barbara Crockett, a nineteen-year-old who had joined the company in 1938, and who danced as one of the four cygnets in this original production, remembered that the dancers didn't know the significance of what they were doing. "Bill said we were going to do *Swan Lake,* so we thought, 'Well, that's great, that's exciting, let's do *Swan Lake.*' It wasn't until afterwards that we realized it was the *first Swan Lake* in the United States and that Bill had never even *seen* the ballet!"

Four years later, for his December 1944 season—and perhaps with the vivid memory of the hundreds turned away from his enormously popular *Swan Lake* as well as from his equally successful 1939 *Coppélia*—Christensen again marked a milestone for American ballet with the first full production of *Nutcracker.* Jocelyn Vollmar, who performed in Willam Christensen's company at age twelve, and who danced in the 1939 *Coppélia* and 1944 *Nutcracker*—shares Crockett's memory of how modestly scaled the young dancers' ambitions were in those path-breaking productions. "I was just excited that I was going to be onstage," Vollmar says. "None of us knew we were making history." Willam Christensen secured a copy of the score from the Library of Congress and asked Russell Hartley, one of his dancers, to design the costumes, which the dancers and their mothers helped sew. Then there was the issue of the choreography. In November, barely a month before the only two *Nutcracker* performances, December 24 and 25 matinees, were scheduled, principal dancer Alexandra Danilova and choreographer George Balanchine arrived in San Francisco on tour with the Ballets Russes de Monte Carlo to perform at the Opera House. Christensen quickly arranged a meeting with them at his apartment, knowing both of them had danced in the Mariinsky Theatre Ballet productions of *Nutcracker* in St. Petersburg. Hartley, who was there as well, recalled that Danilova kicked off her shoes and began dancing every female variation from Clara to the Sugar Plum Fairy for Christensen, but Balanchine quickly stopped her. "No, no Choura, don't show him the steps, let Mr. Christensen do his own choreography!" It turned out to be a prophetic admonition for Christensen's production, which was such an astounding success that it spawned what he called "an epidemic" of ballet companies doing *Nutcrackers* across the United States. Every year since 1944, except one, San Francisco Ballet has performed *Nutcracker.* In 2004 the company premiered Tomasson's lush new production set in 1915 San Francisco.

Dancers' Farewells

One of the ironies of the relationship between repertory and dancers is that the opening of a ballet is always acknowledged while dancers usually begin their careers anonymously, and it is the dancers' *closing* that is publicly noted. Near the end of San Francisco Ballet's 2006 season, four of its best-known dancers retired and were celebrated in two different programs of farewell dancing. Peter Brandenhoff, Stephen Legate, and Yuri Possokhov were featured in an evening of dances tailored to highlight their distinctive relationships to the repertory with excerpts from major works they had danced. "I'm retiring because of the pain," Legate said half in jest in a public interview a few days before the performance. When Megan Low retired a week later, after ten years in the corps de ballet, she said her farewell dancing the lead in Mark Morris's *Sylvia.* Both occasions were marked by a blend of celebration and poignancy. Saying farewell to the company, stage, and dances through which one has grown and defined oneself is the final, and most bittersweet, relationship with repertory that a dancer experiences. Repertory is the means through which a dancer has become visible, and leaving it is how that visibility slips away into memory.

118) Val Caniparoli's
Lambarena (2006)

119 l) Pierre-François
Vilanoba and Sarah Van
Patten in Helgi Tomasson's
Romeo and Juliet (2005)

119 r) Gennadi Nedvigin
in Paul Taylor's *Company B*
(2005)

120–121) Paul Taylor's
Spring Rounds (2006)

122) Tina LeBlanc
and Nicolas Blanc
in George Balanchine's
Square Dance (2005)

123) Kristin Long
as the Black Swan
in Helgi Tomasson's
Swan Lake (2006)

MAKING A BALLET VISIBLE:
REVIVING *RODEO*

Coaxing a ballet back onto the stage from memories, notes, and videos is an imperfect but surprisingly effective process. Ballet Mistress Anita Paciotti is one of San Francisco Ballet's four staff members entrusted with this sensitive and recurrent task. Agnes de Mille's 1944 Americana classic, *Rodeo,* is one of the ballets for which Paciotti is a walking memory bank.

Paciotti's preparations for reviving *Rodeo* began six months before the performance. She checked out a documentary video from the company's archives and gathered her notes from having watched the ballet being staged in 1989. Then she started dancing around in her living room. "It's a big disadvantage if you are setting ballets you never danced," she says.

Although there are formal methods of notating dances, most ballet mistresses use personally devised systems. Paciotti calls hers "stream of consciousness"—pages of scribbled descriptions of the dance steps and where they occur in Aaron Copland's syncopated score for *Rodeo*. She also read portions of de Mille's early writings and noted with amusement that at the ballet's premiere all the dancers portraying wild west cowboys were Russians. "When *we* first did the ballet, Helgi told me, 'Get the Americans in there,'" Paciotti says.

Once she had brought the ballet back into her physical memory, Paciotti taught the steps to the full cast of twenty-one dancers in two weeks. "I got the bones together," Paciotti says. Several weeks later, history arrived in the person of Christine Sarry, one of the finest interpreters of the central role of the Cowgirl, and a dancer taught directly by de Mille.

In Sarry's rehearsals with the company, and particularly the three casts of principal dancers and soloists, Paciotti's bones of *Rodeo* got some meat. One of the pleasures of *Rodeo* is its rich gestural vocabulary, and Sarry worked repeatedly with Cowgirl and principal dancer Kristin Long on something as simple yet resonant as the precise kind of stiff-legged walk that conveys a body weary from hours on horseback or how to snap the torso back and then forward to suggest riding a wildly rearing and then fleeing horse. "It's got to make conversational sense," Sarry told Long. "It works better if you're not imitating the music. It has to have that out-of-control look."

The push for accuracy when a ballet is revived extends beyond the choreography to the smallest details of the costumes. While eight cowhands were learning how to swing imaginary lariats, Patti Fitzpatrick, costume supervisor, was making the rounds of every western shop in a hundred-mile radius looking for just the right cowboy hat to replace a lost one. The following day she discovered the Cowgirl's blue bow had faded to purple. After several attempts to redye the bow, Fitzpatrick began canvassing ribbon stores for a new ribbon of exactly the right color, and by the next day's performance, hats, bows, and steps were all reconstituted.

124) Agnes de Mille's
Rodeo (2006)

125) Ballet Mistress
Anita Paciotti in
rehearsal (2006)

126) Tina LeBlanc (left)
and Anita Paciotti in
Helgi Tomasson's *Giselle*
(2005)

127) Helgi Tomasson's
Romeo and Juliet (1995)

128) (left to right) Parrish
Maynard, Tina LeBlanc,
and Benjamin Pierce in
Julia Adam's *Night* (2001)

129) Molly Smolen in
*Five Brahms Waltzes in the
Manner of Isadora Duncan*
(2007)

6

The Invisible City Backstage

The remarkable thing about being backstage in the Opera House when San Francisco Ballet is in season is noticing how the invisible coexists so closely with the visible. The most public part of a ballet performance—the dancers performing onstage—is always right next to the most private—the bustling city of backstage activity that keeps everything humming. The Opera House itself is constructed like a massive city hall with offices arranged around the perimeter of the four-story auditorium in its midst. This central space is where peerlessly articulate and fluent bodies perform an art that consists of an exquisite balance between what to conceal and what to reveal.

130-131) Costumes
from Yuri Possokhov's
Reflections (2005)

132) A Community
Matinee at the
War Memorial
Opera House (2005)

133

Makeup and Costume Rooms

Below the stage, in the windowless basement of the Opera House, a warren of spare and cramped chambers house the men's and women's wardrobe and costume rooms, the laundry and drying rooms, and the makeup and wig centers for the ballet. Each is staffed by a skillful and steady long-term crew who labor underground, or sometimes in the wings or hallways just outside the dancers' dressing rooms, for the five months a year that the ballet occupies the Opera House. The most they ever see of a performance is a partial view from the wings on a slow night.

On the day of a performance, affable makeup artist Richard Battle's room is usually a dancer's first stop after warming up. Battle, who trained as a watercolorist before becoming head of makeup for the ballet thirty years ago, begins with his staff of five or six makeup artists and hairstylists two hours before the first performance of the day. They clean and arrange the makeup they will use on the dancers and brush out and set any wigs or hair extensions needed for the afternoon's or evening's ballets. If it is a two-performance day and they have already been on duty since an earlier matinee, Battle and his crew will pause at 5:30 P.M. for their union-mandated dinner break before the evening performance. Often they watch a movie Battle supplies, usually a comedy. The room echoes with laughter as they comment on the images on the screen mounted in a corner of the room. In a couple of hours, this same monitor will relay that night's production, played live to backstage and downstairs screens.

During the 2006 production of *Swan Lake,* three shelves of men's elaborate white eighteenth-century wigs sit on wigmaker's heads at one end of the room, waiting for the arrival of the dancers portraying courtiers in Act III. Professional stylist's chairs line both sides of the room in front of mirrored makeup stations. Dozens of pots of powder, cream foundation, eye shadow, eyeliner, mascara, and lipstick and eyelashes sit in neat rows on the counters, ready for the dancers. Many dancers prefer to put on their own makeup in their dressing rooms upstairs, but often the principal dancers or soloists who need special highlighting will stop by to have Battle and his staff prepare them.

Technically the dancers aren't supposed to arrive before 7 P.M., but Battle sympathetically allows Gonzalo Garcia, who will be making his debut this evening as Prince Siegfried, to slip in at 6:45 P.M. while things are still peaceful. Garcia enters quietly, wearing black nylon warm-up pants, a red ribbed sweater, and quilted down boots. He sits silently as Battle explains that because Garcia sweats a lot he should have extra layers of cream base and powder over his face and neck. "Ashley [Wheater] wants me to give you smoky eyes tonight," Battle teases as he applies white contour eye shadow thickly under Garcia's brow and heavy brown shadow along the sides of his nose and in the hollows of his cheeks. "We need this color on your brows—otherwise your eyes will just be like a black pit," he tells Garcia. "But you have a good mouth so I don't need to pencil in your lips."

In ninety minutes Garcia will be dancing one of the most demanding dramatic roles for a male in classical ballet, yet he is composed, polite, courteous, and remarkably self-contained. After Battle completes Garcia's makeup, Garcia moves to the hair stylist's chair across the room. He sits hushed, closing his eyes as his just-washed wavy brown hair is blown dry and then sprayed and shaped into a swept-back look and a little *quequ,* a period ponytail, is attached. "Thank you everyone," Garcia says softly as he leaves to go upstairs and get into his costume. The room is pervaded by a sense of calm and efficiency. It is clear that the entire downstairs staff is there to serve the dancers. For many of them, like Garcia this evening, the transition into performance mode begins with the first application of makeup as they watch their features fade into the accented images of their stage personae. Stage makeup is generally twice as heavy as regular makeup, so when the dancers are viewed up close in the makeup room, their features look exaggerated and harsh, particularly in comparison to the casual warm-up sweats and comfy slippers they wear.

There is an order in which the dancers have their makeup put on. If the performance has children—like *Nutcracker* or *Swan Lake*—they get made up first, escorted in by a volunteer to have a light dusting of color put on their cheeks and lips and to have their hair styled and sprayed. Next the soloists and corps de ballet dancers begin arriving. They rotate through an assembly line of sponges, foundation, rouge bottles, and eyeliner and mascara that a volunteer with BRAVO, the ballet's volunteer service organization, has arranged at one side of the room. The volunteer rinses out the makeup sponges in disinfectant as quickly as the dancers use them. "This is the most normal and happiest place in the building," Battle says.

Backstage is also where a dancer's status within the company is affirmed by the location of his or her dressing room. Shortly before the gala performance a few nights earlier, Garcia had learned that his dressing room for the season would be the only men's one on the coveted stage level and that he would be sharing it with Stephen Legate and Yuri Possokhov, the senior male principal dancers. This was a vivid marker of his ascendancy in rank, which in the lexicon of dressing rooms at the Opera House means down in location. The corps de ballet dancers are in the group of dressing rooms the farthest from the stage high up on the third floor. "When I walked in and saw them, it suddenly hit me," Garcia said. "Oh my God, I'm in *this* dressing room with Yuri and Stephen!"

Across the hall from the makeup room, Patti Fitzpatrick, costume supervisor, who has been maintaining the company's costumes since 1994, works with the wardrobe crew to prepare racks of clean and repaired costumes to deliver to the dancers' dressing rooms half an hour before curtain. Often, if there has been a matinee performance, an entire washer full of tights will be laundered and dried between shows so they are ready in time for the evening performance.

Performances are always layered in the backstage rooms. One performance is always fading out of view as costumes are cleaned and packed away before being moved across town with that production's props and scenery to be stored in the ballet's warehouse. At the same time, another show is coming into view as the crates of its costumes are unpacked and freshened for the opening of the next program. This evening Yuan Yuan Tan's Black Swan tutu for a *Swan Lake* performance later in the week is arranged on a nearby table awaiting some new appliqués. Up close it looks surprisingly plain—its distant dazzle seems to be just gold paint, gold braid, and appliqué illuminated just right by the stage lights. Tonight dresser Muzette Trace, who like Fitzpatrick has her own performing history—appearing for many years with the Shipstads and Johnson Ice Follies—will be stationed at a small table in the hallway outside the principal women's dressing rooms. There, summoned by a dancer poking her head out in the hallway, she can dash inside to help hook a tutu or make some quick stitches on the tutu's hidden leg elastics, sewing them to the ballerina's tights if necessary. The swan tutus for the soloists and corps can have several sets of bars to hook at different settings because up to three casts of dancers share one of these tutus, which range from about $3,000 for a basic one to $5,000 for a fancy one with elaborate ornamentation on top of the basic crinoline, netting, and cotton and rayon bodice.

The Magic in the Wings

Every effort backstage goes toward creating as seamless an onstage image as possible. Generally the more magical the illusion is onstage, the more intense the actions are offstage to maintain it. Sometimes a very quick costume change is needed midperformance—as when Odile dashes offstage as the deceitful Black Swan at the end of the third act of *Swan Lake* and reenters moments later in the fourth act as Odette, the tragically doomed White Swan. Trace, the principal women's dresser, will use a "quick change booth," a temporary dressing room backstage made of wood frames with black fabric stretched across them, and a small chair and table set up inside. There she lays out a dancer's costume, tutu, shoes, and hair ornaments, so she can swiftly strip and dress a dancer in privacy in a matter of seconds while the performance continues a few feet away. Occasionally a hairdresser stands by to help with a hair change as well.

In *Swan Lake*, the evil Sorcerer, von Rothbart, has one such speedy backstage change when he exits in his third-act ballroom attire and does not have time to get to his dressing room before he has to reenter in his soft boots and black winged cape as the owl-like ruler of the swans. The moment von Rothbart steps into the wings on his exit, he is surrounded by two dressers who wear bike lights affixed to elastic bands on their foreheads like miners. Working quickly and noiselessly, they strip off von Rothbart's coat, shoes, pants, and stockings, in this well-rehearsed order, and redress him in his swamp cape and ballet boots. A member of the makeup staff peels off his wig and replaces it with a hard skullcap hairpiece. Another staff member reapplies big birdlike streaks of black liquid makeup on his neck. The von Rothbart tonight, Pierre-François Vilanoba, jumps onto a rock upstage on cue just as the curtain rises and waves his wings menacingly. He quickly exits, and the wardrobe staff surrounds him again, aiming their forehead lights at his ankles so he can finish lacing his boots before dashing back onto the stage for his final death scene of cascading falls as the sincerity of Siegfried and Odette's love destroys him.

When he is backstage, Lee Moffatt, principal dresser, who has worked for the men's wardrobe department since 1992, always wears an emergency fanny pack outfitted with needle, thread, tape, and notepad. In a pinch he can make what he calls "Frankenstein stitches"—"zap, zap, zap, bye!" he says, gesturing in big hurried stitches. Revered for his calm professionalism, Moffatt has even performed emergency sewing while a dancer is still onstage. Working covertly in the midst of a performance, he once darned the split seam on a pair of jeans while the male dancer was wearing them during *Western Symphony*. Moffatt accomplished this by hiding in the scenery immediately behind the cowboy and sewing frantically. "We are there backstage at every performance in case something breaks or goes wrong," he says. "Like the spare tire you pay for and hope you never use."

136) Makeup and
wig artists prepare
Damian Smith for
his role as von Rothbart
in Helgi Tomasson's
Swan Lake (2005)

137) Pauli Magierek
gets ready for a
performance (2003)

Costume Dialogues

A thick layer of work continually undergirds every image of effortlessness and magic in the art on the stage. Like the dancers, ballet costumes must appear ethereal, yet in reality be immensely durable. San Francisco costume designer and fabric artist Sandra Woodall, who has been constructing and designing costumes for San Francisco Ballet since 1976, offers a nuanced commentary on the ballet themes she designs through her costumes. "I like to see the dancers' muscles through their costumes," she says. "It's also all about material and the way in viewing a dance you gather layers of meaning through the intersection of experiences you are having." In creating the scenic design and costumes for Yuri Possokhov's 2005 modernist yet classical *Reflections*, Woodall invented a parallel in costumes—the neoclassical tutu. "I wanted beautifully transparent white tutus for this ballet. So I made costumes that could suggest the idea of a classical treatment of contemporary form," she says. "I designed tutus suggesting the idea of transparency as if showing through to the classical tutu that inspired them." Woodall spoke while viewing a parade of dancers in a fitting for the partially finished costumes she was designing for Helgi Tomasson's *The Fifth Season*.

"*The Fifth Season* is an abstract piece," Woodall says of this ballet named after composer Karl Jenkins's minimalist score that accompanies it. "I think of the costumes and scenic designs as being like the ice you look down on from a plane flying over Greenland." Tomasson first contacted Woodall nearly a year before the ballet's premiere and asked her to design the costumes and simple backdrops. Soon afterward she participated in a special workshop for dyeing fabric, and these new techniques figured in the several dramatic hanging panels with washes of melting earth tones she created for *The Fifth Season*.

In a more literally narrative ballet, such as Tomasson's 2004 restaging of *Nutcracker*, for which he engaged New York costume designer Martin Pakledinaz, the working process can be tightly collaborative. "I think the most important thing is that, like the dance itself or like the music itself, you want to make sure you don't put too much information into your clothing," says Pakledinaz, who has designed three other ballets for Tomasson. "When I'm designing a dance for Helgi I want him to be totally hands-on. As simple as it may seem there were many times during the designing of *Nutcracker* when we had him come in to figure out the skirts for the Snowflakes—the *exact* length on the leg, how many layers of tulle, the fullness of the skirts. It was wonderful to see him come in several times to look at different dancers wearing the tutus and doing bits of dancing for him, so he could go away and really think about whether he wanted a two-inch change in the length or not."

In the last half hour before the curtain rises, the focus of activity moves upstairs from the makeup and costume rooms to backstage, and the tempo accelerates into a countdown mode. The mood is genial but extremely efficient as the stage managers banter with the dancers and production staff while keeping a close eye on the clock on the three backstage monitors. At precisely thirty minutes before the curtain, the first "call" goes out to the dancers, reminding them to sign in with Alan Villareal, the scheduling administrator, and a former dancer with Oakland Ballet. Another warning follows at ten minutes until showtime, alerting the dancers to be onstage and in their places. The orchestra is given a five-minute warning to take their seats in the pit, and Martin West, music director and principal conductor, stands ready to stride to his podium.

Dancers begin collecting around tables on either side of the stage, each one of which holds a supply of onstage essentials: rubbing alcohol in a spray bottle to get pointe shoes to shrink to fit, a bottle of water with a sprayer to stretch overly tight pointe shoes, a jar of Vaseline to coat teeth so the dancers' lips don't stick when they smile, a long metal file to rough up the shank or toe of a pointe shoe, and a large bottle of hand sanitizer for post–pas de deux and partnering hand cleaning.

The backstage chatter quiets to a hushed silence with the first light cue to dim the house lights. The orchestra's individual tuning swells to a uniform harmonizing on the first violinist's A note, and the audience hears the recorded announcement reminding them to turn off cell phones and pagers. For the next two-and-a-half hours, the smooth functioning of months of rehearsals, thousands of hours of preparation, and the collaborative work of nearly two hundred experts will unfold with ordered precision based on each cue from the stage managers. Reading their own copy of a conductor's score for each ballet and watching his downbeat and cues to the orchestra on one of their monitors, they softly call out every lighting, set, and prop change, falling and rising curtain, and even the sequence and timing of the bows for each of the dancers at the ballet's end.

The carpentry, electrical, and prop crews perform a backstage choreography as intricate as that of the dancers. Costumed in black pants and T-shirts, several members of the property crew work throughout the performance on a raised platform, "the rail," at the side of the stage next to dozens of hanging ropes. They labor steadily and silently, "flying" drops and wings in and out by a complex system of pulleys with thirty-pound yellow cement bricks as counterbalances. Set pieces are raced on and off between acts and intermissions as well. The world backstage is animated by highly efficient chaos, right up to the threshold of onstage. This onstage/offstage perimeter can be both rigid and seemingly relaxed, yet every person backstage understands the extraordinary achievement that stepping into the light signifies.

There is sometimes a tendency to think that ballet only reflects society in the era of seventeenth-century courtly etiquette—but it has been steadily contemporized with each passing decade. Among the elements that San Francisco Ballet shows onstage are the highest practices of twenty-first century values: how to be fully in the present moment, how to change to suit the context, how to be clear and sharply legible about who you are. These are the lessons of ballet in the contemporary moment conveyed by the performances of phenomenally fluent bodies.

Joanna Berman recalls that during the years she was a principal dancer with the company she was always aware of the unique depth of her immersion into the character of Giselle and the rare way it extended the enchantment of the stage far into the backstage. "*Giselle* was one of the few ballets in my career where I always kept in character in the wings," Berman says. "It's such a perfect ballet, especially the second act, because you are supposed to be this spirit. I didn't want to interrupt that. So wherever I was, the story continued and every entrance moved the story along. Everyone backstage understood immediately that if you see Giselle walking around you're not going to come over and talk about a great restaurant you just tried."

In the Audience

During intermissions, work of a different nature is occurring upstairs in the box seats. Here the development staff might bring a sociable dancer not performing that evening to be introduced to a corporate sponsor and guests as a means of signifying the type of special access and insider status accorded to sustaining donors to the ballet. On the same floor, Executive Director Glenn McCoy circulates in the private Intermezzo Lounge, discreetly consulting his list of special people to greet that evening as he welcomes patrons and donors during the intermission.

Meanwhile, General Manager Lesley Koenig keeps her focus roving during the performance as she shifts between the audience, the lounge, and backstage. "I just keep moving," she says. "I check in with the house manager, who oversees the audience's experience from arrival to departure, and his team of ushers, ticket takers, coat checkers, taxi hailers, and nurse. I wander through the audience at intermission. I visit the Intermezzo Lounge to greet trustees and meet other donors." Koenig's primary focus, however, is backstage. "It's critical for management to be present everywhere so that all the artists and crew know that we're focused on what they do, and not simply supporting art in our offices behind mounds of paper."

In the same way that the performance onstage both rewards and inspires financial support, another location in the Opera House is very important to the company's solvency. One of the smallest spaces in the building, just off the main exterior lobby, has one of the biggest tasks. Here, in a closet-sized cubicle inside the brass-framed glass entrance doors of the Opera House, most of the San Francisco Ballet's earned revenue is collected by the box office staff that sell tickets throughout the ballet's season. This is effectively the bank for the multilevel "ballet city" that resides backstage, above stage, and under stage in the Opera House. It's also the office of passports to the exceptional experiences and viewing pleasures that wait inside.

The End of the Illusion

All the more remarkable is that the city sustaining this is itself illusory. Within hours of the conclusion of the final performance of the season in May 2006, San Francisco Ballet's full presence in the Opera House is crated up and packed away. Everything—including all the costumes, set pieces, and scenery, every black cloth wing and lighting fixture, the wooden floor built on top of the Opera House stage, every item in each dancer's dressing room down to the name tag on the door—is packed away and stored. Then, in early December, immediately after the conclusion of San Francisco Opera's season, the ballet will move back into the Opera House, and the bustling backstage life of San Francisco Ballet will again become a visible city.

A FINELY TUNED EAR
FOR BALLET

The metaphors Martin West reaches for when describing the relationship of the San Francisco Ballet Orchestra to the company tend toward luxury automobiles. "It's like driving a nice car down the road and adjusting a bit as you drive, avoiding potholes," says West, music director and principal conductor of the orchestra since autumn of 2005. "You try to spot what the dancer is up to and then you help."

Collaboration and troubleshooting from the pit are essential facets of the ballet conductor's role in keeping the stage picture calm and the dancing vibrant and musical. The late Denis De Coteau, the longest tenured conductor of the San Francisco Ballet Orchestra, who led it from 1975 to 1998, used to memorize the season's scores so he could watch the stage during the performance—particularly his favorite ballerina, the sublimely musical Betsy Erickson. British-born West favors the reverse: "I attend to both, the stage and the pit—all the time," he explains. "I watch a lot of rehearsals, so I can visualize the dance in my own head. The less I have to watch the dancers in performance, the more I can just keep the stage in my peripheral vision. Ballet conducting for me involves working with the dancers as if they were a solo musician."

Learning where potential trouble spots might come up is one way to do this. During the company's 2006 summer performances in New York, West, who tours with the company, noticed some difficult spots in the *Don Quixote* pas de deux at the dress rehearsal. Later, when the same thing happened in the performance, he remembered the momentary tricky passage and knew it would smooth out momentarily and that he didn't need to compensate with music. At times a little unpredictability from the pit can be a welcome way to help keep ensemble passages from becoming routine. "So the corps doesn't get in a rut when it is dancing character dances in a long ballet, I might subtly change the tempo just a bit," says West. "It gives them a smile."

Anita Paciotti, one of the company's ballet mistresses, commends the clarity of West's work. "I've never seen anyone who explains music as clearly as Martin," she says. "He has an ear for detail. The orchestra loves him because he is very bright and hands-on. He's like a teacher."

Although he is only thirty-seven, West had ten years of experience conducting for the English National Ballet when he arrived in San Francisco. He is an exacting but playful leader. During a lag in a dress rehearsal, he comically picks up the podium telephone and pretends to order pizza, to the amusement of the full orchestra. The musicians have responded in kind, proffering repeated invitations to West to join their infamous intermission poker game that has been going on for more than two decades in the musicians' lounge below the stage. The problem, says West, who graduated with a degree in mathematics from Cambridge University, is the lack of clear structure. The game is governed by strange rules only the musicians seem to understand.

140) The San Francisco
Ballet Orchestra (2006)

141) Music Director and
Principal Conductor
Martin West in rehearsal
with the San Francisco
Ballet Orchestra (2006)

142) Katita Waldo and
Rory Hohenstein in
Stanton Welch's *Falling*
(2006)

143) Evelyn Cisneros and
Anthony Randezzo in
Geroge Balanchine's
Ballo della Regina (1988)

144–145) Sarah Van Patten
in Helgi Tomasson's
The Fifth Season (2006)

146–147) William Forsythe's
Artifact Suite (2006)

148) Elizabeth Loscavio
and Christopher Stowell in
August Bournonville's
Flower Festival in Genzano
(1991)

149) Katita Waldo in
Mark Morris's *Sylvia*
(2006)

7

Onstage in New York

On a humid Tuesday morning in late July 2006, the largest dance studio on the fifth floor of the New York State Theatre in New York City's Lincoln Center was packed with San Francisco Ballet dancers. At precisely eleven o'clock, Helgi Tomasson strode quickly down the narrow hallway and into the center of the studio. The chatter in the room quieted as attention shifted to the slender figure of Tomasson, who wore jeans, brown loafers, and a black T-shirt with the words "San Francisco Ballet" printed in tiny letters on the front. Stepping to the center of the room, next to a metal barre, he demonstrated the first *demi-plié,* gesturing for a very lifted upper body by brushing his hand upward across his own torso. Almost in a whisper Helgi Tomasson had begun class for the company he built, now on tour, in the theater that built him.

It was an emotional homecoming for Tomasson, who defined himself as a dancer with New York City Ballet dancing on the State Theatre stage, taking class and rehearsing in this studio, daily, for fifteen years. The evening before at a welcome reception at the Alvin Ailey American Dance Theater studios, hosted by James H. Herbert II, co-chair of San Francisco Ballet's board of trustees and executive committee, Tomasson had spoken briefly. He disclosed little about the personal significance of this occasion of the company's fifth tour to New York under his leadership, the second to the State Theatre, other than his personal knowledge of New York's dance standards and his belief that the company would meet and exceed them.

150–151) Outside Paris's National Archives, the site of *Les Etés de la danse* festival (2005)

152) On tour, San Francisco Ballet rehearses at the Harrod Amphitheater in Athens accompanied by Michael McGraw on the piano (2004)

153) Pamela Joyner and James H. Herbert II, co-chairs, San Francisco Ballet board of trustees (2006)

From the start of his tenure in 1985, touring has been an important part of Tomasson's remaking of San Francisco Ballet. In the first twenty years of his leadership, the company toured abroad twelve times, three times as much as it had in the previous fifty years. This international profile is both practical and visionary. Very simply, the company has to tour internationally to be visible in the global dance world. Practically, because the company continues to share its home theater, the War Memorial Opera House, with the San Francisco Opera, and is limited to just five months in this theater each year, major touring is necessary to keep the company's competitive roster of dancers and choreographers busy, gratified, and visible.

Clement Crisp, dance critic for London's *Financial Times* for more than forty years, is one of the many international dance authorities who have seen the company on tour. "They perform tremendously well," says Crisp. "I mean the energy, the clarity, the vitality, that sense of frankness. It's like honesty. They don't lie. San Francisco Ballet tells the truth about dance as they understand it. I think they're absolutely wonderful." Jenny Gilbert, critic for London's *Independent*, agrees. "They've been one hell of a world-class company," she says.

From the opening gala program that kicked off the company's weeklong visit to New York that Tuesday evening in July, it was apparent just how pumped up the San Francisco Ballet dancers were about the tour. Watching Kristin Long, Katita Waldo, and Vanessa Zahorian tear through the women's trio in William Forsythe's *The Vertiginous Thrill of Exactitude* with risky, racing dives onto pointe at the State Theatre made palpable the charge that touring gives the company. New York dance critic Anna Kisselgoff, in reviewing the gala for the online *Voice of Dance,* called the dancing of all three "[a] jaw-dropping exposition in neoclassicism," citing the high energy, daring, and full-force physical virtuosity of their performance. And so it is through the ranks—from star ballerina Tina LeBlanc's vivacity and transparent musicality in George Balanchine's *Harlequinade Pas de Deux* with Joan Boada to corps dancers James Sofranko, Martyn Garside, and Jonathan Mangosing's tightly unison and sleek racing charges across the stage in the third movement from Jerome Robbins's *Glass Pieces.* Touring amplifies a dancer's achievement across audiences, cities, and nations.

154) Tina LeBlanc and Nicolas Blanc rehearse George Balanchine's *Square Dance* for a performance in Paris (2005)

The Ballet Steps Out

San Francisco Ballet was twenty-four years old when it left home for the first time. Invited by the United States Department of State to spend ten weeks in Asia, the company departed in January 1957, becoming the first American ballet company ever to perform in eleven countries: Taiwan, China, Singapore, the Philippines, Indonesia, Cambodia, Thailand, India, Sri Lanka, Myanmar (Burma), and Pakistan. It seems like an odd itinerary for an American company, until one looks at the sponsor and the year. This was the height of the Cold War, and culture—the more youthful, American, and accessible the better— was a weapon. These cities were strategic frontlines for cultural diplomacy against the specter of Soviet influence. Suddenly the American style that San Francisco Ballet had been quietly nurturing had become a potential bulwark against Communism.

Nancy Johnson Carter, a twenty-six-year-old principal dancer with the ballet at the time, remembers the company discreetly being assessed before the tour by a member of the Department of State in late July 1956 at the Jacob's Pillow Dance Festival in Massachusetts during a residency of well-received performances. Before the engagement was over, Ted Shawn, a modern dancer and the director of Jacob's Pillow, wrote an effusive letter to Alfred Frankenstein, critic for the *San Francisco Chronicle* and a member of the dance panel for the Department of State. Shawn praised the company for its unique style and distance from "the distracting and degenerative influences of both New York and Hollywood. Because of the geographical isolation, this company has a pure style, an esprit de corps, a homogeneity that does not exist in any other ballet company resident in the U.S.," he wrote, noting that he found the company similar in spirit to the elegant Royal Danish Ballet because of these qualities.

Within a few weeks Lew Christensen received an invitation from the director of American National Theatre and Academy, which administered the Department of State's international tours, requesting he take his company abroad. However, the invitation came with the stipulations that the company tour with a program of the full-length *Swan Lake* and that guest artist Alexandra Danilova dance the lead. Christensen refused both requests, responding that the company would only tour using its own repertory and its own dancers, bolstered by just one "big name," Leon Danielian, who was nearing the end of his career with the Ballets Russes de Monte Carlo. The dance panel and Department of State agreed.

San Francisco Ballet proudly issued a press release detailing the dancers' preparations of picking up passports and undergoing several weeks of inoculations, as if they were going to some of the most remote corners of the world, which by 1950s standards they were. "We went to countries tourists weren't allowed to visit, countries not even on visas," says Carter, who also went on the company's four-month tour to Latin America the following year and the three-month tour to the Middle East in 1959, the third and final one sponsored by the Department of State. "It wasn't easy traveling but it was as fun as anything and totally unique," she says, her voice rising with excitement as she remembers it fifty years later.

In addition to sold-out enthusiastic audiences and supportive press in every city they visited, Carter recalls the serious challenges of performing in odd venues, while injured or ill, and in difficult climates with impractical heavy Western costumes. Zippers and metal hooks rusted from the constant moisture, legs ached from performing on nonresilient surfaces like badminton courts in Singapore, and nerves were tested in improvised theaters like the Quonset hut in Manila where a sold-out 3,300-seat theater was besieged by another 4,000 people who had also been sold tickets. Principal dancer Sally Bailey recalled dancing in costumes that were perpetually wet so that by the tour's final performances she was wearing a *Nutcracker* tutu now green and smelly with mildew.

Carter says the dancers were coached minimally before they left "in terms of politeness, being conservatively dressed, and learning a word or two in each nation's language." Their role as ambassadors, however, was essentially unscripted, other than being cautioned to avoid controversial political discussions. The dancers' comfort, health, and safety received scant more attention—there were outbreaks of meningitis, armed combat outside the dancers' hotel in one city, persistent suitors for every female dancer, and performing venues that lacked heat, fresh air, and smooth floors.

Leo Diner, the production manager who accompanied the dancers on their foreign tours, carried a movie camera with him on the 1957 tour to Asia. Segments of the surviving footage show cheerfully accommodating dancers wearing full romantic tutus in the wilting heat as they gamely pose atop camels with vistas of the sun-soaked ruins in the distance. They are the classic souvenir images announcing the achievement of travelers to have reached their destination and also indirectly a snapshot of American ballet, barely two decades old and already iconic as an image of the nation's youthfulness, fortitude, and resilience. The Department of State's internal summary of San Francisco Ballet's tour noted "this group was hailed throughout the tour as excellent in public relations work. There was not a word of criticism of offstage conduct, while most posts praised the many fine qualities of the young and vivacious group . . . the company was able to win praise for its dancing and/or its clear message to the citizens of other nations that American young people are interested in them as people, and interested in their language and culture." The critic for Istanbul's *Yeni Sabah* newspaper wrote prophetically: "It would not be a wild dream to anticipate West Berlin, Rome, Paris and London audiences cheering the San Francisco Ballet one day . . . It is very likely that the world might speak in the future of American ballet just as it now speaks of Russian, French and British ballet."

The Rewards of Touring

The vocal acclaim greeting the company on its return was striking. Carter recalls proclamations, receptions at San Francisco City Hall, press conferences, media attention, and a mayoral gathering and greetings at the airport. Here was an ensemble of young people—the average age of the company on the first tour was nineteen—whose mere presence and performing were seen as emblematic of the nation as they traveled by problematic transport to distant and challenging locales.

The benefits of travel proved substantial for the company. Beyond the immediate gains of increased ticket sales and visibility, the ballet had its own simple agenda for the advantages of touring: more paid employment, more attention, and much more adventure. The Jacob's Pillow performances had been the first time the company performed in the eastern United States; its previous tours had been generally limited to smaller cities in the West. In 1955 the company danced only thirty-seven performances in San Francisco, and the staff worried constantly about the handful of leading dancers leaving for bigger companies or a living wage. It's remarkable that even in the twenty-first century some of these same concerns continue to motivate the company to tour.

Being a small and portable company had been an important factor in the Department of State's selection of San Francisco Ballet for international touring. In 1960, a few months after the company's final sponsored tour abroad, another small ballet troupe with a strong level of performance was being auditioned by the dance panel in its summer performances at Jacob's Pillow. The company was approved, and preparations began for it to tour under government auspices to Jordan, Syria, Lebanon, Iraq, Iran, Afghanistan, India, and Egypt. This company was the Joffrey Ballet, and its newest male dancer, who had just been hired in time for the tour, was a promising young Icelandic native, Helgi Tomasson.

"We had marvelous tours," Tomasson recalls, referring to the Joffrey's extensive December 1962 to March 1963 tour to the Middle East and India and the October 1963 tour to the Soviet Union. These major international tours marked Tomasson's first experiences as a professional dancer with an American company. The Joffrey took twenty-six dancers to the Soviet Union with a repertory weighted toward contemporary and modern dance works but also including August Bournonville's pas de deux from *Flower Festival in Genzano*, which Tomasson danced with Marlene Rizzo, giving the Russians their first sample of Bournonville. A few months after arriving in New York, Tomasson had become part of the largest program of dance diplomacy ever launched in the United States. He was now a cultural ambassador of American ballet, a commission he would spend the rest of his life fulfilling as a dancer, international ballet competitor, choreographer, and eventually artistic director.

When San Francisco Ballet tours in the twenty-first century, union rules protect the dancers from the travails of cold theaters and damp costumes, but touring still brings challenges, some of them remarkably similar to those from the company's first ventures. Ashley Wheater, ballet master and assistant to the artistic director, recounts the continuing tensions between programming what a sponsor wants and what the artistic director would like to show off about the company. "There was one time when we were planning to go on tour and the sponsor wanted a full-length ballet, in a city where they had seen many, many full lengths," Wheater says. "Helgi didn't want to do that. He wanted to take a repertory that would show the company and show the world what we are doing. It ended up that he got his way and people were amazed by the depth of the repertory. It's very hard on the company in a week to do eleven different ballets. But in that eleven ballets you're showing every different facet of your company, and you're trying to get every single dancer on stage, instead of a full length, which really just features two people."

Then there is the issue of finances. Taking one hundred and twelve people—the minimal group of dancers, technicians, and support staff the ballet tours with—to Europe for several weeks is expensive, particularly since the Department of State ceased covering the costs decades ago. In 1997 philanthropist Richard N. Goldman, a member of the board of trustees, responded to Tomasson's need to tour by creating a special fund so that the ballet could plan touring over a multi-year time frame. Support comes in other ways as well. Longtime trustee Lucy Jewett and her husband, Fritz Jewett, often follow the company on tour, and they have created an in-house ritual of hosting a party for the full company whenever it goes abroad. These have been lavish events such as taking over one of the trendiest nightclubs in Paris for an all-night party at the conclusion of the 2000 Paris tour, and in the summer of 2005 chartering buses to transport the company and staff to a private luncheon in Claude Monet's gardens in Giverny.

The dancers have their own set of touring challenges. Joanna Berman recalls having to dance *Swan Lake* in London in 1999 after several nights of jet-lagged sleeplessness. "I remember just sitting in my dressing room at the Sadler's Wells Theatre and crying because I had gotten so little sleep and couldn't catch up because of the time difference," Berman says. "But the *Swan Lake* performances went great—I don't know why. But I found touring more and more stressful as I got older," Berman continues. "When I first joined the company it was so wonderful to have that as your job. But jet-lag was the hardest part of international touring."

In the 1960s and 1970s, when San Francisco Ballet was considerably smaller with only thirty dancers most of the time, touring added to the group's sense of cohesiveness and camaraderie. Allyson Deane, who danced with the company from the mid-1960s to the early 1980s, recalls company tours as times when the divide between directors and dancers loosened. "I remember Lew Christensen teaching us all to walk backwards into the ocean once when we were on tour in Hawaii," Deane says. "There he was with his flippers on," she laughs as she demonstrates how the distinguished white-haired choreographer humorously rounded up the dancers and began choreographing this rear advance into the waves.

Costume Supervisor Patti Fitzpatrick, part of the core staff who always tour with the company, says that for her touring is about three things: "laundry, cleaning, and arranging costumes." She always brings along the company's own washer and dryer, as the costumes are too important to trust to unknown equipment. One of her worst touring experiences was the company's 1999 tour to Tivoli Gardens in Copenhagen where the staff was unfailingly helpful and assured Fitzpatrick that she could leave the washer and dryer at home. She obeyed, but with the first load of wash Fitzpatrick discovered to her horror that European washer/dryer machines were hot and impossible to stop midcycle. The entire company's tights and unitards had to be washed by hand and dried with fans each night for the whole engagement so that they did not disintegrate.

Touring the Neighborhood

Beginning in 1979, San Francisco Ballet initiated a new domestic touring program—very domestic touring—to neighborhoods of San Francisco. Instead of the dancers of the company, these tours feature the exuberant and passionate Charles Chip McNeal, the ballet's dedicated director of education, and the staff of ten dance teachers and musicians he has trained to teach weekly introductory classes in twenty-seven public schools. Founded on the belief that dance is a basic expression of the pleasure of rhythmic movement and should be available to underserved young people as an important part of the city's community life, the San Francisco Ballet Center for Dance Education operates out of second-floor offices in the ballet's Franklin Street building.

Articulate and messianic about the virtues of dance education, McNeal trained in ballet, tap, and folkloric dance before developing San Francisco Ballet's community outreach and education programs in 1979. As the company's education ambassador, McNeal begins a typical day in the multipurpose room at an early morning dance class at Hillcrest Elementary School in the city's low-income Bay View–Hunters Point neighborhood. There, while overseeing a teacher having a difficult day, McNeal steps in to model for him how to keep the class on course and the students' excitement about dance alive. "Look at you! You have creativity just waiting to burst through," he eagerly greets a boy he secretly deems a potential distraction to the class, enlisting him immediately as his special helper. "If you think you are going to fall down, control your body," he tells another. "I want you to be safe," he cautions, leading the students into a game about how to be near and far from the other students in the class as they cultivate a new awareness of their bodies in space and, most critically, their power over shaping their bodies' actions. Afterward, back in his office, McNeal heads a lunch meeting about approving a teacher study guide that he and former principal dancer Evelyn Cisneros-Legate have written.

The afternoon finds McNeal, a large, muscular man with dreadlocks down his back who moves with the easy grace of a former dancer, leading the first of two late afternoon scholarship classes for two dozen eight- and nine-year-old girls in a third-floor studio in the ballet building. These are lessons alike in kind, but different in objective, from those taught in the San Francisco Ballet School studios just across the hall where young dancers are being instructed into compliance with the strictures of ballet. "Access, education, opportunity" is McNeal's mantra as he turns his attention toward his studio filled with little girls in black leotards and pink tights and ballet shoes, all supplied by the ballet as part of the scholarship program. "Don't look football player-ish," he jokes with them, and they soften their arms into gentle circles as they practice step-pivot-step-pivot *chaînés tours* turns across the studio.

"The dual purpose of this program is to inform and support the diverse students with potential," McNeal says. "Half of the students who come through this program are boys and half are nonwhite. Even those who don't have the right feet to do ballet should have the opportunity to have a professional dance experience of this kind so then they can choose another kind. The important thing is that this brings them into the world of dance."

Several weeks later in May 2006, at the close of the school year, a sampling of students from the ballet's Dance in Schools and Communities program are gathered excitedly in the grand North Light Court of San Francisco's City Hall for a mini-showcase hosted by Mayor Gavin Newsom. In the same space that five months earlier was filled with hundreds of the ballet's major donors at an elegant dinner celebrating the opening of the repertory season, an assortment of family members and friends from the community now cheer enthusiastically for the students from the city's alternative public schools as they perform dances they have helped create to the accompaniment of music from the SFJAZZ high school ensemble.

The real partners in this afternoon's performance—the early immigrants, benefactors, audiences, and generations of dancers and choreographers—are no longer visible, but their legacy is an enduring awareness of San Francisco Ballet as a cultural jewel in the city's life. In tandem with this awareness is a vision of the clarity and dynamism of the fine-tuned dancing body of classical ballet and the possibilities for a civically and aesthetically enriched life it continues to model and inspire.

158–159) San Francisco Ballet rehearses George Balanchine's *Apollo* at the Harrod Amphitheater in Athens, Greece (2004)

161) Cyril Pierre and Lucia Lacarra in Helgi Tomasson's *Handel—A Celebration* (1998)

THOSE TINY
SATIN PEDESTALS

Shoes—they are the bane of every female dancer's existence and the fulcrum and tiny pedestal that displays her achievement. When San Francisco Ballet goes on tour, shoes are the most important item every ballerina packs and the last one she can determine. "You need a lot of shoes," says Joanna Berman, a former principal dancer and veteran of many tours. Berman remembers the frustration of trying to pack the big theater cases every dancer receives two weeks before leaving on tour. "It's great because the company ships the case for you in advance. But packing is awful because it's so hard to determine what shoes to bring."

In place of most travelers' shoe quandary about style or color, the dancer's dilemma has to do with number and noisiness. "A lot of women try on several pairs of pointe shoes to pack for each different ballet they will be dancing," Berman says. "You might need a perky one for *The Sleeping Beauty* or a pliable one for a ballet where you don't want to make any noise when you run. A dancer can easily go through two pairs of pointe shoes a day on tour, particularly if you are doing really hard ballets and having a dress rehearsal every day."

The nuances of how old and quiet or new and loud pointe shoes are can be critical when a dancer is on tour and her supply is back in San Francisco. At home each member of the company receives twelve pairs of ballet shoes a month, paid for by San Francisco Ballet. The shoes are stacked neatly in small personal cabinets in a converted office called the shoe room on the third floor of the ballet building. The person in charge is a former wearer of pointe shoes herself, Sherri LeBlanc. LeBlanc, who retired as a soloist in 2004, is the shoe administrator and the person who orders shoes, ribbons, glue, and elastic for the company's thirty-five women dancers. Asked how it feels to be surrounded by everyone's pain, since women's toe shoes are notoriously uncomfortable, LeBlanc laughs, "I'm just glad I'm not putting them on *my* feet anymore."

162) The company
rehearsing at the
Harrod Amphitheater
in Athens (2004)

163) San Francisco
Ballet on a visit to
Claude Monet's gardens
in Giverny, France
(2005)

164–165) San Francisco
Ballet on tour at the
Lincoln Center Festival
(2006)

Ballets in the San Francisco Ballet Repertory

Title	Choreographer	Composer	SF Ballet Premiere	World Premiere
Arlecchinata	Adolph Bolm	Jean-Joseph Cassanéa de Mondonville	1933	1928
Au Jardin des Tuileries	Adolph Bolm	Johann Strauss	1933	1933
Le Ballet Mécanique (also known as Spirit of the Factory or Iron Foundry)	Adolph Bolm	Alexander Mossolov	1933	1931
Carnival	Adolph Bolm	Nicolai Rimsky-Korsakov	1933	1933
Don Juan	Adolph Bolm	Issac Albéniz	1933	1933
Passacaglia	Adolph Bolm	Cyril Scott	1933	1933
Perpetuum Mobile	Adolph Bolm	Franz Ries	1933	1933
Les Précieux	Adolph Bolm	Sergei Prokofiev	1933	1933
Prelude and Four-Voice Fugue	Adolph Bolm	Johann Sebastian Bach	1933	1933
Reverie	Adolph Bolm	Frédéric Chopin	1933	1933
Roundelay	Adolph Bolm	Kurt Schindler	1933	1933
Voices of Spring	Adolph Bolm	Robert Schumann and Franz Liszt	1933	1933
Abnegation	Adolph Bolm	Isaac Albéniz	1934	1934
Bumble-Bee	Adolph Bolm	Nicolai Rimsky-Korsakov	1934	1934
Caprice Viennoise	Michel Fokine	Fritz Kreisler	1934	1934
Faunesque	Adolph Bolm	Claude Debussy	1934	1934
Hopak	Adolph Bolm	Modest Mussorgsky	1934	1934
Hyde Park Satire	Iris de Luce	Alexander Tcherepnin	1934	1934
Jota Aragonaise	Guillermo del Oro	Camille Saint-Saëns	1934	1934
Lament	Adolph Bolm	Johann Sebastian Bach	1934	1934
Patterns	Adolph Bolm	Alexander Tcherepnin	1934	1934
Pedro the Dwarf	Adolph Bolm	John Alden Carpenter	1934	1934
Raymonda: Grand Pas Espagnol Classique	Adolph Bolm after Marius Petipa	Alexander Glazounov	1934	1934
The Rivals	Adolph Bolm	Henry Eichheim	1934	1925
Wiener Blut	Adolph Bolm	Johann Strauss	1934	1934
El Amor Brujo	Vicente Escudero	Manuel de Falla	1935	1935
Consecration	Adolph Bolm	Johann Sebastian Bach	1935	1935
Cordoba	Vicente Escudero	Isaac Albéniz	1935	1935
Country Dance	Adolph Bolm	Ludwig van Beethoven	1935	1935
Cuadro Flamenco	Guillermo del Oro	Popular	1935	1935
Danse Noble	Adolph Bolm	Johann Sebastian Bach	1935	1935
Firebird: A Solo	Adolph Bolm	Igor Stravinsky	1935	1935
Jota Argonesa	Guillermo del Oro	Louis Moreau Gottschalk	1935	1935
Juris Fanatico	Adolph Bolm	Johann Sebastian Bach	1935	1935
Rondo Capriccioso	Adolph Bolm	Felix Mendelssohn	1935	1935

1933

San Francisco Ballet Landmarks

The San Francisco Opera Association establishes the San Francisco Opera Ballet under the direction of Ballet Master Adolph Bolm, and the War Memorial Opera House opens.

1937

Serge Oukrainsky replaces Adolph Bolm as ballet master.

Willam Christensen, founder of Portland Ballet, organizes San Francisco Ballet's first California tour.

1938

Willam Christensen becomes the company's ballet master. The company performs throughout California and tours the Pacific Northwest, its first venture outside the state.

Title	Choreographer	Composer	SF Ballet Premiere	World Premiere
Russian Peasant Scene	Nicolai Vasilieff	Anatole Liadov	1935	1935
Scheherezade	Adolph Bolm	Nicolai Rimsky-Korsakov	1935	1935
Capriccio Espagnol	Willam Christensen	Nicolai Rimsky-Korsakov	1937	1935
Chopinade	Willam Christensen	Frédéric Chopin	1937	1935
Dance Divertissements	Willam Christensen	Helen Green, Arthur Honegger, and Johannes Brahms (and various folk music)	1937	1937
Encounter (Excerpts)	Lew Christensen	Wolfgang Amadeus Mozart	1937	1936
Rumanian Wedding Festival (also Rumanian Rhapsody)	Willam Christensen	Georges Enesco	1937	1936
Sketches	Willam Christensen	Charles Gounod and Franz Schubert	1937	1937
Ballet Impromptu	Willam Christensen	Johann Sebastian Bach	1938	1938
The Bartered Bride (Three Dances)	Willam Christensen	Bedřich Smetana	1938	1938
In Vienna or In Old Vienna	Willam Christensen	Johann Strauss	1938	1938
A Midsummer Night's Dream	Lew Christensen	Felix Mendelssohn	1938	1938
Romeo and Juliet	Willam Christensen	Peter Ilyich Tchaikovsky	1938	1938
L'Amant Rêve	Willam Christensen	Carl Maria von Weber	1939	1939
American Interlude	Willam Christensen	Godfrey Turner	1939	1939
Coppélia	Willam Christensen	Léo Delibes	1939	1939
And Now the Brides	Willam Christensen	Fritz Berens	1940	1940
A Midsummer Night's Dream	Willam Christensen	Felix Mendelssohn	1940	1940
Swan Lake	Willam Christensen	Peter Ilyich Tchaikovsky	1940	1940
Amor Espanol	Willam Christensen, Elena Imaz, and Maclovia Ruiz	Jules Massenet	1942	1942
Coeur de Glace	Willam Christensen	Wolfgang Amadeus Mozart	1942	1936
Scenes de Ballet	Willam Christensen	Various Composers	1942	1942
Winter Carnival	Willam Christensen	Johann and Josef Strauss	1942	1942
Blue Bird (Pas de Deux)	Marius Petipa	Peter Ilyich Tchaikovsky	1943	1890
Hansel and Gretel	Willam Christensen	Engelbert Humperdinck	1943	1943
Nutcracker Divertissements	Willam Christensen	Peter Ilyich Tchaikovsky	1943	1943
Sonata Pathetique	Willam Christensen	Ludwig van Beethoven	1943	1943
Le Bourgeois Gentilhomme	Willam Christensen, Earl Riggins, and André Ferrier	Jean-Baptiste Lully and André Grétry	1944	1944
Nutcracker	Willam Christensen	Peter Ilyich Tchaikovsky	1944	1944
Triumph of Hope	Willam Christensen	César Franck	1944	1944
Blue Plaza	Willam Christensen and José Manero	Aaron Copland	1945	1945
Pyramus and Thisbe	Willam Christensen	Fritz Berens	1945	1945
Black Swan Pas de Deux	Marius Petipa	Peter Ilyich Tchaikovsky	1947	1895
Dr. Pantalone	Willam Christensen	Domenico Scarlatti	1947	1947
Fantasia	Bronislava Nijinska	Franz Schubert and Franz Liszt	1947	unknown
Giselle	Anton Dolin after Jean Coralli and Jules Perrot	Adolphe Adams	1947	1940/1841
Henry VIII	Rosella Hightower	Gioacchino Rossini Adapted and arranged by Robert Zeller	1947	1947
The Lady of the Camellias	Anton Dolin	Guisseppi Verdi Arranged by Robert Zeller	1947	1947
Mephisto	Adolph Bolm	Franz Liszt	1947	1947
Parranda	Willam Christensen	Morton Gould	1947	1947

1939

San Francisco Opera Ballet presents its first full-length production, *Coppélia*, choreographed by Willam Christensen. It is the first time in this century that an American has choreographed the complete ballet.

1940

San Francisco Opera Ballet presents the first full-length American production of *Swan Lake*.

Willam Christensen's brother Harold is appointed director of the San Francisco Opera Ballet School.

1942

The ballet becomes independent of the Opera and is renamed San Francisco Ballet. The San Francisco Ballet Guild is established to support the company. Willam Christensen becomes director of San Francisco Ballet.

1944

San Francisco Ballet launches a new celebrated holiday tradition that sweeps the country with America's first complete production of *Nutcracker*.

Ballets in the San Francisco Ballet Repertory (continued)

Title	Choreographer	Composer	SF Ballet Premiere	World Premiere
Don Quixote (Pas de Deux)	Marius Petipa	Léon Minkus	1948	1869
Gift of the Magi	Simon Semenoff	Lukas Foss	1948	1945
Persephone	John Taras	Robert Schumann	1948	1948
Les Sylphides	Michel Fokine	Frédéric Chopin	1948	1909
Danza Brillante	Willam Christensen	Felix Mendelssohn	1949	1949
Jinx	Lew Christensen	Benjamin Britten	1949	1942
The Story of a Dancer	Lew Christensen	George Frideric Handel	1949	1949
Vivaldi Concerto (later called Balletino)	Willam Christensen	Antonio Vivaldi	1949	1949
Charade or The Debutante	Lew Christensen	Various Composers	1950	1939
Nothin' Doin' Bar	Willam Christensen	Darius Milhaud	1950	1950
Prelude To Performance	Lew Christensen	George Frideric Handel	1950	1950
Divertimenti	Willam Christensen and Lew Christensen	Peter Ilyich Tchaikovsky	1951	1951
Filling Station	Lew Christensen	Virgil Thomson	1951	1938
Le Gourmand	Lew Christensen	Wolfgang Amadeus Mozart	1951	1951
Les Maitresses de Lord Byron	Willam Christensen	Franz Lizst	1951	1951
American Scene	Lew Christensen	Carter Harman	1952	1952
The Carnival of the Animals	Aaron Girard	Camille Saint-Saëns	1952	1952
Serenade	George Balanchine	Peter Ilyich Tchaikovsky	1952	1935
À la Françaix	George Balanchine	Jean Françaix	1953	1951
Con Amore	Lew Christensen	Gioacchino Rossini	1953	1953
Concerto Barocco	George Balanchine	Johann Sebastian Bach	1953	1941
The Festival	Lew Christensen	Wolfgang Amadeus Mozart	1953	1953
Swan Lake	George Balanchine	Peter Ilyich Tchaikovsky	1953	1951
Beauty and The Shepherd	Lew Christensen	Christoph Willibald von Gluck	1954	1954
The Dryad	Lew Christensen	Franz Schubert	1954	1954
Heuriger	Lew Christensen	Wolfgang Amadeus Mozart	1954	1954
Nutcracker	Lew Christensen	Peter Ilyich Tchaikovsky	1954	1954
Sylvia Pas de Deux	George Balanchine	Léo Delibes	1954	1950
Apollo (originally Apollon Musagete)	George Balanchine	Igor Stravinsky	1955	1928
Renard (The Fox)	Lew Christensen	Igor Stravinsky	1955	1947
The Tarot	Lew Christensen	Peter Ilyich Tchaikovsky	1955	1955
Emperor Norton	Lew Christensen	Vernon Duke	1957	1957
Mendelssohn Concerto	William Dollar	Felix Mendelssohn	1957	1957
Beauty and the Beast	Lew Christensen	Peter Ilyich Tchaikovsky	1958	1958
Lady of Shalott	Lew Christensen	Arthur Bliss	1958	1958
Caprice	Lew Christensen	Franz von Suppé	1959	1959
Danses Concertantes	Lew Christensen	Igor Stravinsky	1959	1959
Divertissement d'Auber (I)	Lew Christensen	François Esprit Auber	1959	1959
Sinfonia	Lew Christensen	Luigi Boccherini	1959	1959
Danza Brillante	Lew Christensen	Felix Mendelssohn	1960	1960
La Esmeralda (Pas de Deux)	Lew Christensen	Cesare Pugni	1960	1960
Pas de Dix	George Balanchine	Alexander Glazounov	1960	1955
Variations de Ballet	Lew Christensen	Alexander Glazounov	1960	1960
Original Sin	Lew Christensen	John Lewis	1961	1961

1951

Lew and Willam Christensen are named co-directors of San Francisco Ballet.

Selections from several of the company's ballets are presented during the first season of Standard Hour Television Broadcasts.

1952

Willam Christensen moves to Salt Lake City to found a ballet department at the University of Utah.

1954

Lew Christensen is appointed San Francisco Ballet's new director. He establishes an exchange policy with New York City Ballet, allowing Balanchine ballets to enter the San Francisco Ballet repertory for the first time.

San Francisco Ballet prepares a second, more elaborate version of Nutcracker. It is entirely re-choreographed by Lew Christensen and set in the American Victorian style of the 1850s. This second production plays for fourteen years, to over 400,000 people.

Title	Choreographer	Composer	SF Ballet Premiere	World Premiere
La Ronde	Michael Smuin	Timothy Thompson	1961	1961
St. George and the Dragon	Lew Christensen	Paul Hindemith	1961	1961
Symphony in C	George Balanchine	Georges Bizet	1961	1947
Jest of Cards	Lew Christensen	Ernest Křenek	1962	1962
Divertissement d'Auber (II)	Lew Christensen	François Esprit Auber	1963	1963
Fantasma	Lew Christensen	Sergei Provkofiev	1963	1963
Gayne (Pas de Deux)	Nina Anisimova Reproduced by Rudolf Nureyev	Anna Khachaturian	1964	1942
Le Corsaire (Pas de Deux)	After Marius Petipa Rudolf Nureyev	Riccardo Drigo and Léon Minkus	1964	1899
The Set	Ron Poindexter	Dave Brubeck	1964	1963 (Workshop)
The Seven Deadly Sins	George Balanchine	Kurt Weill	1964	1958
Shadows	Lew Christensen	Paul Hindemith	1964	1961 (Workshop)
The Sleeping Beauty Grand Pas de Deux	Marius Petipa	Peter Ilyich Tchaikovsky	1964	1890
La Sylphide, Act II (Excerpts)	After August Bournonville Reproduced by Rudolf Nureyev	Herman Løvenskjold	1964	1836
Life, a do-it-yourself disaster (later called *Life A Pop Art Ballet*)	Lew Christensen	Charles Ives	1965	1965
Lucifer	Lew Christensen	Paul Hindemith	1965	1965
Octet	Willam Christensen	Igor Stravinsky	1965	1958
Alpenfest	Carlos Carvajal	Wolgang Amadeus Mozart	1966	1966
Pas de Six	Lew Christensen	Hans Christian Lumbye	1966	1966
Scotch Symphony	George Balanchine	Felix Mendelssohn	1966	1952
Wajang	Carlos Carvajal	Colin McPhee	1966	1966
Way Out (II)	Robert Gladstein	Igor Stravinsky and Georg Reidel	1966	1966
Kromatika	Carlos Carvajal	William Walton	1967	1967
Nutcracker	Lew Christensen	Peter Ilyich Tchaikovsky	1967	1967
Symphony in D	Lew Christensen	Luigi Cherubini	1967	1967
Totentanz	Carlos Carvajal	Warner Jepson	1967	1967
Il Distratto	Lew Christensen	Franz Josef Haydn	1969	1967 (Workshop)
Mobile	Tomm Ruud	Aram Khachaturian	1969	1969 (Workshop)
Night in the Tropics	John Clifford	Louis Moreau Gottschalk	1969	1969
Le Corsaire (Pas de Deux)	Alexander Gorsky	Riccardo Drigo and Léon Minkus	1970	1970
Genesis '70	Carlos Carvajal	Terry Riley	1970	1970
Joyous Dance	Carlos Carvajal	Johann Sebastian Bach	1970	1970
Matinee Dansante	Carlos Carvajal	Gioachino Rossini and Benjamin Britten	1970	1970
Schubertiade	Michael Smuin	Franz Schubert	1970	1970
Split	John Butler	Morton Subotnick	1970	1970
Airs de Ballet	Lew Christensen	André Grétry	1971	1971
Classical Symphony	Leo Ahonen	Sergei Prokofiev	1971	1971
Jon Lord-Both Sides Now	Robert Gladstein	Jon Lord	1971	1971
La Source	George Balanchine	Léo Delibes	1971	1968
Celebration	Robert Gladstein	Alexandre Luigini	1972	1972
La Favorita	Soili Arvola	Gaetano Donizetti	1972	1971 (Workshop)
Figures in F	Jocelyn Vollmar	Gian Carlo Menotti	1972	1972

169

1956

The company makes its East Coast debut at Jacob's Pillow Dance Festival in Lee, Massachusetts, bringing San Francisco Ballet its first national exposure.

1957

The State Department sponsors San Francisco Ballet on an eleven-nation Asian tour. It is the first time an American ballet company performs in East Asia. This is followed by tours of the Middle East and South America.

1960

After a third international tour, the company returns to San Francisco and focuses on establishing a stable home base. During the next twelve years, San Francisco Ballet moves into several theaters in an attempt to find a home.

Ballet '60 becomes one of the first workshops for young choreographers in America.

1964

ABC-TV films *Nutcracker* at the War Memorial Opera House and broadcasts the ballet on New Year's Eve.

Title	Choreographer	Composer	SF Ballet Premiere	World Premiere
N.R.A.	Robert Gladstein	Warner Jepson	1972	1972
New Flower	Carlos Carvajal	Traditional Indonesian Music	1972	1972
Tchaikovsky Pas de Deux	George Balanchine	Peter Ilyich Tchaikovsky	1972	1960
Tingel-Tangel-Taenze	Lew Christensen	Various Composers	1972	1972
Cinderella	Lew Christensen and Michael Smuin	Sergei Prokofiev	1973	1973
Don Juan	Lew Christensen	Joaquin Rodrigo	1973	1973
The Eternal Idol	Michael Smuin	Frédéric Chopin	1973	1969
Harp Concerto	Michael Smuin	Carl Reinecke	1973	1973
Pas de Quatre	Keith Lester and Anton Dolin	Cesare Pugni	1973	1941
The Shakers	Doris Humphrey	Doris Humphrey	1973	1931
Tealia	John McFall	Gustav Holst	1973	1973
The Beloved	Lester Horton	Judith Hamilton	1974	1948
The Dying Swan	Michel Fokine	Camille Saint-Saëns	1974	1905
Flower Festival at Genzano (Pas de Deux)	August Bournonville	Holger Simon Paulli and Edvard Helsted	1974	1858
The Four Temperaments	George Balanchine	Paul Hindemith	1974	1946
Legende	John Cranko	Henri Wienawski	1974	1973
Mother Blues	Michael Smuin	William Russo	1974	1974
Pulcinella Variations	Michael Smuin	Igor Stravinsky	1974	1968
La Sonnambula	George Balanchine	Vittorio Rieti after Vincenzo Bellini	1974	1946
Les Sylphides	Michel Fokine Staged by Alexandra Danilova	Frédéric Chopin	1974	1909
Taming of the Shrew (Pas de Deux)	John Cranko	Kurt-Heinz Stolze	1974	1969
Cry	Alvin Ailey	Alice Coltrane, Laura Nyro, and the Voices of East Harlem	1975	1971
For Valery Panov	Michael Smuin	Sergei Rachmaninoff	1975	1973 (Workshop)
Giselle (Pas de Deux)	After Jules Perrot and Jean Coralli	Adolphe Adam	1975	1841
Harlequinade (Pas de Deux)	Valery Panov after Marius Petipa	Riccardo Drigo	1975	1900
Lady and the Hooligan (Pas de Deux)	Valery Panov after Konstantin Boyarsky	Dimitri Shostakovich	1975	1962
Shinju	Michael Smuin	Paul Seiko Chihara	1975	1975
Adagio Celebre	Valery Panov	Thommaso Albinoni	1976	1976
Afternoon of a Faun	Jerome Robbins	Claude Debussy	1976	1953
Agon	George Balanchine	Igor Stravinsky	1976	1957
Les Chansons de Bilitis	Carmen de Lavallade	Claude Debussy	1976	1976
Garden of Love's Sleep	John McFall	Aram Khachaturian	1976	1976
Heart of the Mountain	Valery Panov	Murad Kozhalyev	1976	1976
Norwegian Moods (originally Stravinsky Pas de Deux)	Lew Christensen	Igor Stravinsky	1976	1976
Opus I	John Cranko	Anton von Webern	1976	1965
Romeo and Juliet	Michael Smuin	Sergei Prokofiev	1976	1976 (Excerpts presented in 1975)
Scott Joplin Rag	Michael Smuin	Scott Joplin	1976	1976
Songs of Mahler	Michael Smuin	Gustav Mahler	1976	1976
Souvenirs	Todd Bolender	Samuel Barber	1976	1955
Beethoven Quartets	John McFall	Ludwig van Beethoven	1977	1977
Firebird	Maurice Béjart	Igor Stravinsky	1977	1970
Gershwin	Robert Gladstein	George Gershwin	1977	1977

1965

San Francisco Ballet debuts in New York City at the New York State Theatre in Lincoln Center.

1967

Lew Christensen presents his new version of Nutcracker, the third production in the company's history.

1968

A one-hour version of Lew Christensen's Beauty and the Beast is broadcast by ABC-TV.

1972

San Francisco Ballet is reorganized. Its various components—the school, company, and guild—now fall under the auspices of a single organization, the San Francisco Ballet Association.

The War Memorial Opera House becomes San Francisco Ballet's permanent home for performing.

Title	Choreographer	Composer	SF Ballet Premiere	World Premiere
The Ice Maiden	Lew Christensen	Igor Stravinsky	1977	1977
Medea	Michael Smuin	Samuel Barber	1977	1977
Metamorphoses	Tomm Ruud	Paul Creston	1977	1977
Moves	Jerome Robbins	In Silence	1977	1959
Peter and the Wolf	Jerome Weiss	Sergei Prokofiev	1977	1977
The Referee	Julie Arenal	Galt MacDermot	1977	1977
Scherzo	Michael Smuin	Gustav Mahler	1977	1977
Sousa March	Michael Smuin	John Philip Sousa	1977	1977
Three	John Butler	Alberto Ginastera	1977	1977
Bach Duet (Puppenspiel)	Michael Smuin	Johann Sebastian Bach	1978	1978
Chi Mai	Robert Gladstein	Ennio Morricone	1978	1978
David and Goliath	Robert North and Wayne Sleep	Carl David	1978	1975
La Fille mal gardée (The Badly Guarded Daughter)	Sir Frederick Ashton	Ferdinand Hérold Freely adapted and arranged by John Lanchbery from the 1928 version	1978	1960
Mozart's C Minor Mass	Michael Smuin	Wolfgang Amadeus Mozart	1978	1978
Orpheus-Return to the Threshold	Jerome Weiss	Alan Hovhaness	1978	1978
Q.a V. (Quattro a Verdi)	Michael Smuin	Giuseppe Verdi	1978	1978
Quanta	John McFall	Dmitri Shostakovich	1978	1978
San Francisco Tango	Michael Smuin	Gus Kahn	1978	1978
Stravinsky Capriccio for Piano and Orchestra	Robert Gladstein	Igor Stravinsky	1978	1978
Trilogy	Tomm Ruud	Béla Bartók and Aram Khachaturian	1978	1978
Allegro Brillante	George Balanchine	Peter Ilyich Tchaikovsky	1979	1956
Circus Polka	Jerome Robbins	Igor Stravinsky	1979	1972
Divertimento No. 15	George Balanchine	Wolfgang Amadeus Mozart	1979	1956
Duettino	Michael Smuin	Giuseppe Verdi	1979	1979
The Mistletoe Bride (2nd Version)	Robert Gladstein	Paul Seiko Chihara	1979	1979
La Rêve de Cyrano	John McFall	Joaquin Nin Culmell	1979	1979
Richmond Diary	Tomm Ruud	Ron Daum	1979	1979
Scarlatti Portfolio	Lew Christensen	Domenico Scarlatti Orchestrated by Benjamin Lees	1979	1979
A Song for Dead Warriors	Michael Smuin	Charles Fox	1979	1979
We, the Clown	John McFall	Victor Charles	1979	1978
Canti	John McFall	Henri Lazarof	1980	1980
Introduction and Allegro	Tomm Ruud	Sir Edward Elgar	1980	1980
Psalms	Robert Gladstein	Leonard Bernstein	1980	1980
The Tempest	Michael Smuin	Paul Seiko Chihara after Henry Purcell	1980	1980 (Excerpts presented in 1979)
Bartók Quartet No. 5	Betsy Erickson	Béla Bartók	1981	1981
Bouquet	Michael Smuin	Dmitri Shostakovich	1981	1981
Debut	Michael Smuin	Alessandro Scarlatti	1981	1981
Monotones I	Sir Frederick Ashton	Erik Satie	1981	1966
Monotones II	Sir Frederick Ashton	Erik Satie	1981	1965
Stars and Stripes	George Balanchine	John Philip Sousa Music adapted and orchestrated by Hershy Kay	1981	1958
Vivaldi Concerto Grosso	Lew Christensen	Antonio Vivaldi	1981	1981

1973

Michael Smuin returns from American Ballet Theatre to accept the position as San Francisco Ballet's associate artistic director. To celebrate the new partnership, Smuin and Christensen collaborate on a full-length production of *Cinderella*.

1974

San Francisco Ballet Association faces bankruptcy. An extraordinary grassroots effort, Save Our Ballet, focuses national attention on the company and launches a new era of creative energy.

1975

A new era of financial stability for San Francisco Ballet begins with the appointment of Dr. Richard E. LeBlond Jr. as president and general manager of the association.

Harold Christensen, director of San Francisco Ballet School, retires after a thirty-five-year tenure.

The company establishes its own resident orchestra under Music Director and Conductor Denis de Coteau.

Ballets in the San Francisco Ballet Repertory (continued)

Title	Choreographer	Composer	SF Ballet Premiere	World Premiere
Badinage	John McFall	Igor Stravinsky	1982	1982
The Dream (Pas de Deux)	Sir Frederick Ashton	Felix Mendelssohn	1982	1964
Love-Lies-Bleeding	Val Caniparoli	Igor Stravinsky	1982	1982
Requiem Canticles	Jerome Robbins	Igor Stravinsky	1982	1972
Steps for Two	Tomm Ruud	Igor Stravinsky	1982	1982
Stravinsky Piano Pieces	Michael Smuin	Igor Stravinsky	1982	1982
Swan Lake—Act II	Kent Stowell after Lev Ivanov	Peter Ilyich Tchaikovsky	1982	1976
Symphony in Three Movements	Robert Gladstein	Igor Stravinsky	1982	1982
Vilzak Variations	Anatole Vilzak after Marius Petipa	Various Composers	1982	1982
Chaconne	George Balanchine	Christoph Willibald von Gluck	1983	1976
Chansons de Sheherazade	Val Caniparoli	Maurice Ravel	1983	1983
Erik Bruhn Master Class in Concert	Erik Bruhn	Various Composers	1983	1983
Forgotten Land	Jiří Kylián	Benjamin Britten	1983	1981
Pixelage	Betsy Erickson	Arcangelo Corelli	1983	1983
Romantic Pieces	John McFall	Antonín Dvořák	1983	1983
Romanze	Michael Smuin and Francis Ford Coppola	Antonín Dvořák	1983	1983
Western Symphony	George Balanchine	Hershy Kay	1983	1954
Cloudless Sulphur	Kirk Peterson	Morton Subotnick	1984	1984
Manifestations	Arthur Mitchell	Primous Fountain III	1984	1975
Mozart Piano Concerto #21	Michael Smuin	Wolfgang Amadeus Mozart	1984	1984
Pigs and Fishes	Elisa Monte	Glenn Branca	1984	1981
Prodigal Son	George Balanchine	Sergei Prokofiev	1984	1929
Signatures	Robert Gladstein	Billy Goldenberg	1984	1984
To the Beatles	Michael Smuin	The Beatles	1984	1984
Troy Game	Robert North	Brazilian Folk Music and Bob Downes	1984	1974
Windows	Val Caniparoli	Ludwig van Beethoven	1984	1984
Brahms/Haydn Variations	Michael Smuin	Johannes Brahms	1985	1985
Brahms-Schoenberg Quartet	George Balanchine	Johannes Brahms Orchestrated by Arnold Schoenberg	1985	1966
Hamlet and Ophelia, pas de deux	Val Caniparoli	Bohuslav Martinů	1985	1985
In the Night	Jerome Robbins	Frédéric Chopin	1985	1970
Lear	Victoria Morgan	Aaron Copland	1985	1985
Menuetto	Helgi Tomasson	Wolfgang Amadeus Mozart	1985	1984
A Midsummer Night's Dream	George Balanchine	Felix Mendelssohn	1985	1962
Othello	Kirk Peterson	Carl Ruggles	1985	1985
Papillon	Eliot Feld	Jacques Offenbach	1985	1979
Bizet Pas de Deux	Helgi Tomasson	Georges Bizet	1986	1986
Concerto in d: Poulenc	Helgi Tomasson	Francis Poulenc	1986	1986
Confidencias	Helgi Tomasson	Ernesto Nazareth	1986	1986
Contredanses	Helgi Tomasson	Ludwig van Beethoven	1986	1984
Hearts (Le Ballet des Couers)	Michael Smuin	Paul Seiko Chihara	1986	1986
Nutcracker	Lew Christensen Additional choreography and staging by Willam Christensen and Helgi Tomasson	Peter Ilyich Tchaikovsky	1986	1986
Opus 19 / The Dreamer	Jerome Robbins	Sergei Prokofiev	1986	1979

1976

Michael Smuin becomes co-artistic director of San Francisco Ballet with Lew Christensen.

1978

Michael Smuin's *Romeo and Juliet* becomes the first full-length American ballet to be broadcast on PBS.

San Francisco Ballet debuts at the Brooklyn Academy of Music.

1979

San Francisco Ballet establishes the Dance In Schools and Communities program to provide a means of access, education, and opportunity for students of diverse cultural backgrounds to experience dance.

1980

Michael Smuin creates *The Tempest*, the first full-length American ballet with original choreography, music, and designs.

Title	Choreographer	Composer	SF Ballet Premiere	World Premiere
Sunset	Paul Taylor	Sir Edward Elgar	1986	1983
La Sylphide	August Bournonville Production directed by Peter Martins	Herman Løvenskjold	1986	1836
Tarantella	George Balanchine	Louis Moreau Gottschalk	1986	1964
Theme and Variations	George Balanchine	Peter Ilyich Tchaikovsky	1986	1947
Ballo Della Regina	George Balanchine	Giuseppe Verdi	1987	1978
The Concert (or, the Perils of Everybody)	Jerome Robbins	Frédéric Chopin	1987	1956
Dreams of Harmony	James Kudelka	Robert Schumann	1987	1987
Intimate Voices	Helgi Tomasson	Niels W. Gade	1987	1987
Narcisse	Val Caniparoli	Claude Debussy	1987	1987
New Sleep	William Forsythe	Thom Willems	1987	1987
Rubies	George Balanchine	Igor Stravinsky	1987	1967
La Sylphide	August Bournonville New production directed by Helgi Tomasson	Herman Løvenskjold	1987	1836
Ballet d'Isoline	Helgi Tomasson	André Messager	1988	1983
Calcium Light Night	Peter Martins	Charles Ives	1988	1977
Duo Concertant	George Balanchine	Igor Stravinsky	1988	1972
Giuliani: Variations on a Theme	Helgi Tomasson	Mauro Giuliani	1988	1984
Polonaise Défilé	Helgi Tomasson	Antonín Dvořák	1988	1988
The Sons of Horus	David Bintley	Peter McGowan	1988	1985
Swan Lake	Helgi Tomasson after Marius Petipa and Lev Ivanov	Peter Ilyich Tchaikovsky	1988	1988/1895 (Petipa-Ivanov)
The Comfort Zone	James Kudelka	Ludwig van Beethoven	1989	1989
Connotations	Val Caniparoli	Benjamin Britten	1989	1989
Handel—A Celebration	Helgi Tomasson	George Frideric Handel	1989	1989
In the Middle, Somewhat Elevated	William Forsythe	Thom Willems	1989	1987
Interplay	Jerome Robbins	Morton Gould	1989	1945
Pas de Trois (Glinka)	George Balanchine	Mikhail Glinka	1989	1955
Reflections of Saint Joan	Helgi Tomasson	Norman Dello Joio	1989	1989
Rodeo	Agnes de Mille	Aaron Copland	1989	1942
Con Brio	Helgi Tomasson	Riccardo Drigo	1990	1990
Harvest Moon	Lisa de Ribère	As arranged for the Glenn Miller Orchestra	1990	1990
In Perpetuum	Val Caniparoli	Arvo Pärt	1990	1990
Krazy Kat	Brenda Way	Jelly Roll Morton, Charles L. Roberts, and William Bolcom	1990	1990
Rodin	Leonid Jacobson	Claude Debussy and Alban Berg	1990	1958
The Sleeping Beauty	Helgi Tomasson after Marius Petipa	Peter Ilyich Tchaikovsky	1990	1890
Tagore	Glen Tetley	Alexander von Zemlinsky	1990	1989
Valses Poeticos	Helgi Tomasson	Enrique Granados	1990	1990
The "Wanderer" Fantasy	David Bintley	Franz Schubert Arranged for orchestra and piano by Franz Liszt	1990	1990
Aurora Polaris	Helgi Tomasson	Johann Sebastian Bach	1991	1991
Bugaku	George Balanchine	Toshiro Mayuzumi	1991	1963
Dark Elegies	Anthony Tudor	Gustav Mahler	1991	1937
"Haffner" Symphony	Helgi Tomasson	Wolfgang Amadeus Mozart	1991	1991

1981

PBS's "Dance in America" series presents Michael Smuin's The Tempest, the first ballet broadcast live from the War Memorial Opera House. The broadcast, co-produced by KQED San Francisco and WNET New York, wins an Emmy Award for the company.

The company makes its Western European debut at the Edinburgh International Festival.

San Francisco Ballet School is chosen by the Prix de Lausanne, the prestigious international ballet competition held in Switzerland, as one of seven schools to which the award-winning dancers are sent for training.

1983

San Francisco Ballet, the oldest professional ballet organization in America, is the first major American dance company to celebrate its 50th anniversary.

San Francisco Ballet moves into a $13.8 million home: the first building in the history of American dance created expressly to house a major professional dance institution.

Ballets in the San Francisco Ballet Repertory (continued)

Title	Choreographer	Composer	SF Ballet Premiere	World Premiere
Meistens Mozart (originally Mostly Mozart)	Helgi Tomasson	Wolfgang Amadeus Mozart, Karl von Dittersdorf, Jakob Haibl, and Bernhard Flies	1991	1991
Napoli (Divertissements from Act III)	August Bournonville	Holger Simon Paulli and Edvard Helsted	1991	1842
Paquita (Pas de Deux)	Lola de Avila after Marius Petipa	Léon Minkus	1991	1881
Pulcinella	Val Caniparoli	Igor Stravinsky	1991	1991
Tryst	Val Caniparoli	Wolfgang Amadeus Mozart	1991	1991
Beads of Memory	Helgi Tomasson	Peter Ilyich Tchaikovsky	1992	1985
The End	James Kudelka	Johannes Brahms	1992	1992
Forevermore	Helgi Tomasson	Antonín Dvořák	1992	1992
Job	David Bintley	Ralph Vaughn Williams	1992	1992
Le Quattro Stagioni (The Four Seasons)	Helgi Tomasson	Antonio Vivaldi	1992	1992
Two Plus Two	Helgi Tomasson	Gioacchino Rossini	1992	1992
Who Cares?	George Balanchine	George Gershwin Lyrics by Ira Gershwin	1992	1970
Aunis	Jacques Garnier	Maurice Pacher	1993	1979
Company B	Paul Taylor	Songs sung by The Andrew Sisters	1993	1991
Little Waltz	Helgi Tomasson	Eric Coates	1993	1985
Nanna's Lied	Helgi Tomasson	Kurt Weill and Friedrich Hollaender	1993	1993
La Pavane Rouge	Redha	Tape collage	1993	1993
Seeing Stars	Val Caniparoli	Ernö von Dohnányi	1993	1993
The Dance House	David Bintley	Dmitri Shostakovich	1994	1994
Gumbo Ya-Ya	Donald McKayle	James Newton	1994	1994
In G Major	Jerome Robbins	Maurice Ravel	1994	1975
Maelstrom	Mark Morris	Ludwig van Beethoven	1994	1994
Quartette	Helgi Tomasson	Antonín Dvořák	1994	1994
Romeo and Juliet	Helgi Tomasson	Sergei Prokofiev	1994	1994
Sighing Land	Anna Laerkesen	Jean Sibelius	1994	1994
La Esmeralda (Pas de Deux)	After Julies Perrot	Cesare Pugni	1995	1844
Die Fledermaus, Act II (Waltz)	Helgi Tomasson	Johann Strauss Jr.	1995	1990
Lambarena	Val Caniparoli	Johann Sebastian Bach and traditonal African music (as arranged by Pierre Akendenqué and Hughes de Courson)	1995	1995
Pacific	Mark Morris	Lou Harrison	1995	1995
Sonata	Helgi Tomasson	Sergei Rachmaninov	1995	1995
Stravinsky Violin Concerto	George Balanchine	Igor Stravinsky	1995	1972
Terra Firma	James Kudelka	Michael Torke	1995	1995
Tuning Game	Helgi Tomasson	John Corigliano	1995	1995
When We No Longer Touch	Helgi Tomasson	Kristopher Anthony	1995	1995
Back Home	Dietmar Seyffert	Gustav Mahler	1996	1996
Drink To Me Only with Thine Eyes	Mark Morris	Virgil Thomson	1996	1988
A Fleeting Moment	David Palmer	Béla Bartók	1996	1996
Fly by Night	Christopher d'Amboise	Steven Bernstein	1996	1996
The Lesson	Flemming Flindt	Georges Delerue	1996	1963
Maninyas	Stanton Welch	Ross Edwards	1996	1996
Soirées Musicales	Helgi Tomasson	Benjamin Britten	1996	1996

1984

Lew Christensen is the first recipient of the Lew Christensen Medal to honor the company's 50th anniversary in recognition of his lifelong service to the company. The award is not annual and is reserved to honor individuals who have left an indelible mark on San Francisco Ballet.

Board of Trustees member L. Jay Tenenbaum is also awarded the medal in recognition of his leadership in fund-raising for the San Francisco Ballet Building fund.

San Francisco Ballet debuts at the Spoleto Festival in Italy and then makes an extensive five-week tour to Italy, Israel, and Greece.

Lew Christensen, America's first "premier danseur" and respected colleague of George Balanchine, dies.

Michael Smuin is named principal guest choreographer.

Michael Smuin's A Song For Dead Warriors airs on PBS's "Dance in America" series, and receives an Emmy Award for direction and choreography.

Title	Choreographer	Composer	SF Ballet Premiere	World Premiere
The Waltz Project	Peter Martins	Various Composers	1996	1988
La Cathédrale Engloutie	Stanton Welch	Claude Debussy	1997	1997
Ciao, Marcello	Val Caniparoli	Nino Rota	1997	1997
Criss-Cross	Helgi Tomasson	Domenico Scarlatti (as arranged by Charles Avison) and Arnold Schoenberg (after Handel)	1997	1997
Flames of Paris (Pas de Deux)	Vassili Vainonen	Boris Assafiev	1997	1932
Four Last Songs	Ben Stevenson	Richard Strauss	1997	1980
El Grito (The Cry)	Lila York	Dietrich Buxtehude, Chico O'Farrill, Luis Gianneo, Oscar Lorenzo Fernandez, and Alberto Ginastera	1997	1997
Pandora Dance	Helgi Tomasson	Aaron Jay Kernis	1997	1997
Sergeant Early's Dreams	Christopher Bruce	Traditional Folk Songs	1997	1984
Shogun (to my Grandfather)	Ivonice Satie	Milton Nascimento and Fernando Brant	1997	1982
Aria	Val Caniparoli	George Frideric Handel	1998	1997
The Cage	Jerome Robbins	Igor Stravinsky	1998	1951
Études	Harald Lander	Knudage Riisager after Carl Czerny	1998	1948
Glass Pieces	Jerome Robbins	Philip Glass	1998	1983
Grande Pas Classique	Victor Gsovsky	François Esprit Auber	1998	1949
Liebeslieder Walzer	George Balanchine	Johannes Brahms	1998	1960
Othello: A Dance in Three Acts	Lar Lubovitch	Elliot Goldenthal	1998	1997
Paquita (Pas de Trois)	Lola de Avila after Marius Petipa	Léon Minkus	1998	1881
Silver Ladders	Helgi Tomasson	Joan Tower	1998	1998
Slow	Val Caniparoli	Graham Fitkin	1998	1998
Some Women and Men	James Kudelka	Francis Poulenc	1998	1998
Twilight	Helgi Tomasson	Felix Mendelssohn	1998	1998
Two Bits	Helgi Tomasson	Aaron Jay Kernis	1998	1998
The Vertigious Thrill of Exactitude	William Forsythe	Franz Schubert	1998	1996
William Tell (Pas de Deux)	August Bournonville	Gioacchino Rossini	1998	1842
Adagio for Strings	Gerard Bohbot	Samuel Barber	1999	1991
Aquilarco	Val Caniparoli	Giovanni Sollima	1999	1999
Chaconne for Piano and Two Dancers	Helgi Tomasson	George Frideric Handel	1999	1999
Gala Performance	Anthony Tudor	Sergei Prokofiev	1999	1938
Giselle	Helgi Tomasson after Marius Petipa, Jules Perrot, and Jean Coralli	Adolphe Adam Additional music, orchestrations and arrangements by Freidrich Bürgmuller, Ludwig Minkus, and Emil De Cou	1999	1999/1841
The Invitation	Kenneth MacMillan	Matyas Seiber	1999	1962
Sandpaper Ballet	Mark Morris	Leroy Anderson	1999	1999
Solo	Hans van Manen	Johann Sebastian Bach	1999	1997
A Suite of Dances	Jerome Robbins	Johann Sebastian Bach	1999	1994
Taiko	Stanton Welch	Sen Amano, Michael Askill, Ian Cleworth, Rebecca Lagos, and Colin Piper	1999	1999
Vestris	Leonid Jacobson	Genaidi Banschikov	1999	1969
Celts	Lila York	The Chieftains, Mason Daring, William J. Ruyle, Bill Whelan, Celtic Thunder	2000	1996
Concerto Romantique	David Palmer	Max Bruch	2000	2000

1985

San Francisco Ballet appears in two national television broadcasts: KQED's television production of Lew Christensen's *Jinx*; and a Great Performances "Dance in America" broadcast of Lew Christensen and Michael Smuin's *Cinderella*.

The company debuts at the John F. Kennedy Center for the Performing Arts in Washington, DC.

Helgi Tomasson, premier danseur of New York City Ballet, becomes artistic director and choreographer of San Francisco Ballet.

1986

Helgi Tomasson's debut season as artistic director of San Francisco Ballet features several of his own works, including *Concerto in d: Poulenc, Confidencias, Contredanses,* and *Menuetto.*

The season is launched by a lavish, new full-length production of *Nutcracker*, the fourth production in the company's history.

Ballets in the San Francisco Ballet Repertory (continued)

Title	Choreographer	Composer	SF Ballet Premiere	World Premiere
Impetuous	Vladimir Anguelov	Philip Glass	2000	2000
The Kingdom of the Shades from *La Bayadère, Act II*	Natalia Makarova after Marius Petipa	Ludwig Minkus Orchestration by John Lanchbery	2000	1980
Magrittomania	Yuri Possokhov	Yuri Krasavin after Ludwig van Beethoven	2000	2000
*Much Ado . . . * (Excerpt)	Helgi Tomasson	Sir Arthur Sullivan	2000	1999
Night	Julia Adam	Matthew Pierce	2000	2000
Opus 50	Christopher Stowell	Peter Ilyich Tchaikovsky	2000	2000
Pas de Deux (from *Proust*) adapted from Marcel Proust's *A la Recherche du Temps Perdu*	Roland Petit	Camille Saint-Saëns	2000	1974
Raymonda, Act III	Rudolf Nureyev after Marius Petipa	Alexander Glazounov	2000	1983
Sea Pictures	Christopher Wheeldon	Edward Elgar	2000	2000
Symphony in Three Movements	George Balanchine	Igor Stravinsky	2000	1972
L'Arlésienne	Roland Petit	Georges Bizet	2001	1974
Black Cake	Hans van Manen	Igor Stravinsky, Jules Massenet, Pietro Mascagni, Leos Janácek, and Peter Ilyich Tchaikovsky	2001	1989
Death of a Moth	Val Caniparoli	Carlos Surinach	2001	2001
Fanfare	Jerome Robbins	Benjamin Britten	2001	1953
A Garden	Mark Morris	Richard Strauss after François Couperin	2001	2001
Liebestod	Gerard Bohbot	Richard Wagner	2001	2000
Prism	Helgi Tomasson	Ludwig van Beethoven	2001	2000
Revelation	Motoko Hirayama	John Williams	2001	2000
Without Words	Nacho Duato	Franz Schubert	2001	1998
Angelo	Julia Adam	Antonio Vivaldi	2002	2002
Bartók Divertimento	Helgi Tomasson	Béla Bartók	2002	2002
Chi-Lin	Helgi Tomasson	Bright Sheng	2002	2002
Continuum	Christopher Wheeldon	György Ligeti	2002	2002
Damned	Yuri Possokhov	Maurice Ravel	2002	2002
Dances at a Gathering	Jerome Robbins	Frédéric Chopin	2002	1969
Jewels	George Balanchine	Gabriel Fauré, Igor Stravinsky, and Peter Ilyich Tchaikovsky	2002	1967
Later	Mark Morris	Franz Schubert	2002	2002
Light Rain (Excerpt)	Gerald Arpino	Douglas Adams	2002	1981
No Other	Val Caniparoli	Richard Rodgers	2002	2002
Paquita	Natalia Makarova after Marius Petipa	Ludwig Minkus Orchestrated by John Lanchbery with additional music by Riccardo Drigo and Nicolai Tscherepnin	2002	1980/1847
Le Carnaval des Animaux	Alexei Ratmansky *The Dying Swan* after Mikhail Fokine	Camille Saint-Saëns	2003	2003
Concerto Grosso	Helgi Tomasson	Francesco Geminiani	2003	2003
Don Quixote	Alexander Gorsky and Marius Petitpa. Staging and additional choreography by Helgi Tomasson and Yuri Possokhov	Ludwig Minkus	2003	2003/1869
Elite Syncopations	Sir Kenneth MacMillan	Scott Joplin and Various Composers	2003	1974
imaginal disc	Julia Adam	Matthew Pierce	2003	2003
Polyphonia©	Christopher Wheeldon	György Ligeti	2003	2001
Rush©	Christopher Wheeldon	Bohuslav Martinů	2003	2003

1987

The company completes a Pacific Rim tour in the fall, which includes performances in Tokyo and Singapore.

Richard E. LeBlond Jr., president of the San Francisco Ballet Association from 1975 to 1987, is awarded the Lew Christensen Medal.

1988

San Francisco Ballet presents the world premiere of Helgi Tomasson's full-length ballet *Swan Lake*.

Wayne Prim, chairman of the executive committee, board of trustees, 1973 to 1987, is awarded the Lew Christensen Medal.

1989

San Francisco Ballet performs Tomasson's *Swan Lake* as part of the Festival de Paris.

1990

San Francisco Ballet presents the world premiere of Helgi Tomasson's full-length ballet *The Sleeping Beauty*.

W. McNeil Lowry, president of San Francisco Ballet, 1988 to 1991, is awarded the Lew Christensen Medal.

Title	Choreographer	Composer	SF Ballet Premiere	World Premiere
There Where She Loved © (originally There Where She Loves)	Christopher Wheeldon	Frédéric Chopin and Kurt Weill	2003	2000
Tu Tu	Stanton Welch	Maurice Ravel	2003	2003
7 for Eight	Helgi Tomasson	Johann Sebastian Bach	2004	2004
Grosse Fuge	Hans van Manen	Ludwig van Beethoven	2004	1971
Nutcracker	Helgi Tomasson	Peter Ilyich Tchaikovsky	2004	2004
Square Dance	George Balanchine	Antonio Vivaldi and Arcangelo Corelli	2004	1957
Study in Motion	Yuri Possokhov	Alexander Scriabin	2004	2004
Sylvia: A Ballet in Three Acts	Mark Morris	Léo Delibes	2004	2004
Symphonic Variations	Sir Frederick Ashton	César Franck	2004	1946
Thaïs Pas de Deux	Sir Frederick Ashton	Jules Massenet	2004	1971
Bagatelles	Helgi Tomasson	Béla Bartók	2005	2005
Dybbuk	Jerome Robbins	Leonard Bernstein	2005	1974
Elemental Brubeck ©	Lar Lubovitch	Dave Brubeck	2005	2005
Falling	Stanton Welch	Woflgang Amadeus Mozart	2005	2005
Quaternary ©	Christopher Wheeldon	John Sebastian Bach, John Cage, Arvo Pärt, and Steven Mackey	2005	2005
Reflections	Yuri Possokhov	Felix Mendelssohn	2005	2005
Sin Regreso	Myriam Agar	Philip Glass	2005	2004
"...smile with my heart" ©	Lar Lubovitch	Marvin Laird after Richard Rodgers	2005	2002
Spring Rounds	Paul Taylor	Richard Strauss	2005	2005
Afternoon of a Faun	Jerome Robbins	Claude Debussy	2006	1953
Artifact Suite	William Forsythe	Johann Sebastian Bach and Eva Crossman-Hecht	2006	2004
Blue Rose	Helgi Tomasson	Elena Kats-Chernin	2006	2006
Chopiniana (Pas de Deux)	Michel Fokine	Frédéric Chopin	2006	1908
Harlequinade Pas de Deux	George Balanchine	Riccardo Drigo	2006	1955
The Fifth Season	Helgi Tomasson	Karl Jenkins	2006	2006
Other Dances	Jerome Robbins	Frédéric Chopin	2006	1976
Carousel (A Dance) ©	Christopher Wheeldon	Richard Rodgers Arranged and orchestrated by William David Brohn	2007	2002
Concordia	Matjash Mrozewski	Matthew Hindson	2007	2007
Eden/Eden	Wayne McGregor	Steve Reich	2007	2005
Fancy Free	Jerome Robbins	Leonard Bernstein	2007	1944
Firebird	Yuri Possokhov	Igor Stravinsky	2007	2007
On Common Ground	Helgi Tomasson	Ned Rorem	2007	2007

177

1991

San Francisco Ballet performs at City Center Theater in New York City, the company's first New York appearance in twenty-six years.

1992

Helgi Tomasson is awarded the *Dance Magazine* Award, as well as the American Academy of Achievement Golden Plate Award.

San Francisco Ballet School attends the ballet festival Recontres Internationales de la Danse de la Baule in France—the only American ballet school to receive this prestigious invitation.

1993

San Francisco Ballet is the first professional ballet company in America to celebrate its 60th anniversary. Founder and Honorary Gala Chairman Willam Christensen attends the opening night celebration and receives a standing ovation.

Current Artists of the Company

Artistic Director

Helgi Tomasson

Principal Dancers

Nicolas Blanc
Joan Boada
Lorena Feijoo
Gonzalo Garcia
Tiit Helimets
Davit Karapetyan
Tina LeBlanc
Kristin Long
Muriel Maffre
Ruben Martin
Pascal Molat
Gennadi Nedvigin
Damian Smith
Molly Smolen
Yuan Yuan Tan
Sarah Van Patten
Pierre-François Vilanoba
Rachel Viselli
Katita Waldo
Vanessa Zahorian

Principal Character Dancers

Ricardo Bustamante
Val Caniparoli
Jorge Esquivel
Anita Paciotti

Soloists

Elana Altman
Garrett Anderson
Frances Chung
Jaime Garcia Castilla
Rory Hohenstein
Moises Martin
Elizabeth Miner
Nutnaree Pipit-Suksun
Hansuke Yamamoto

Corps de Ballet

Dores Andre
David Arce
Brett Bauer
Maureen Choi
Courtney Clarkson
Diego Cruz
Daniel Deivison
Courtney Elizabeth
Hayley Farr
Martyn Garside
Dana Genshaft
Nicole Grand
Adeline Kaiser
Margaret Karl
Pauli Magierek
Brian Malek
Jonathan Mangosing
Alexandra McCullagh
Andrea McGinnis
Erin McNulty

Joanna Mednick
Alexandra Meyer-Lorey
Brooke Taylor Moore
Steven Norman
Chidozie Nzerem
Mariellen Olson
Aaron Orza
Patricia Perez
Joseph Phillips
Shannon Roberts
Lily Rogers
Miriam Rowan
Danielle Santos
Garen Scribner
James Sofranko
Anthony Spaulding
Jennifer Stahl
Benjamin Stewart
Matthew Stewart
Quinn Wharton
Courtney Wright
Kirill Zaretskiy

Apprentices

Gaetano Amico
Ludmilla Campos
Sasha De Sola
Christopher Mondoux

Ballet Master/Assistant to the Artistic Director

Ashley Wheater

Ballet Mistresses

Betsy Erickson
Anita Paciotti

Ballet Master

Ricardo Bustamante

Choreographer in Residence

Yuri Possokhov

Music Director and Principal Conductor

Martin West

Artistic Directors, 1933–2008

Adolph Adam, 1933–1937
Willam Christensen, 1938–1951
Lew Christensen, 1951–1984
Michael Smuin (Co-Artistic Director), 1976–1984
Helgi Tomasson, 1985–present

Lists of Artists, Board of Trustees, Orchestra, and Staff (178–186) current as of April 15, 2007.

Artists of the Company, 1933–2007

(App.) = Apprentice
(G.A.) = Guest Artist

Name	joined	Name	joined	Name	joined
Abbe, Tilly/Matilda	1956	Bauer, Brett	2002	Broughton, Brooke	1997
Abbott, Betty Scoble/Elizabeth	1933	Beattie, Katherine	1944	Broulette, Julienne	1936
Ackerman, Maile	1967	Beckwith, Barbara	1939	Browning, Virginia	1934
Adam, Julia	1988	Begany, Barbara	1964	Brox, Gerard	1971
Adams, Barbara	1953	Belerue, Mary	1936	Bruce, Bob	1964
a.k.a. Johnston, Barbara		Bell, Bonnie	1944	Brumbley, June	1933
Adamson, Sandra	1968	Bell, Robert E.	1933	Brunette, Ms.	1943
Adler, Louise	1937	Bello Portu, Jean-Baptiste	1990	Bucher, Gerrie	1957
Agnese, Rita	1962	Benichou, Pascal	1985	Buck, Webster	1950
Ahonen, Leo	1968	Bennet, Joan	1941	Bugbee, Donna	1934
Aitken, Peter	1943	Bennett, Christine	1966	Bujones, Fernando (G.A.)	1976/1977
Albertsen, Victoria	1934	Bennett, Damara	1971	Burgess, Richard	1943
Albertson, Alaina	1986	Bennett, Ruth	1937	Burgess, Walter	1949
Alden, Guy	1933	Berci, Vadja	1936	Burnett, Jackie	1943
Alden, Walter	1934	a.k.a. del Oro, Vadja		Burr, Mary	1937
Alexandrova, Galina	1989	Berg, Henry	1963	a.k.a. Carruthers, Mary; Tovanya, Maria	
Alfieri, Claudia	1997	Bergman, Alan	1966		
Allan, Edward	1936	Bering, Christine	1951	Busch, Christine	1973
Allemann, Sabina	1988	Berkins, Cosette	1936	Bustamante, Ricardo	1981
Allen, Dennis	1964	Berman, Joanna	1984	Butler, Daryl	1971
Allen, Willette	1937	Bernal, Tina	1962	Butt, Miriam	1935
Altman, Elana	2001	Bernard, Lois	1940		
Alvarez, Mariana	1973/1977	Berry, Lynda	1962	Caccialanza, Gisella	1943
Amico, Gaetano (App.)	2006	Bertch, Bonnie	1940	Callow, Charlene	1955
Anderson, Christopher	1986	Bialoblocki, Patricia	1968	Campos, Ludmila (App.)	2006
Anderson, David	1962	Bibbins, Patricia	1947	Cancilla, Gloria	1952
Anderson, Garrett	2001	a.k.a. Johnston, Patricia		Cane, Jean	1935
Andre, Dores	2004	Bickmore, Rex	1964	a.k.a. Dalziel, Jean	
Andrews, Jon	1947	Bilz, Nell	1933	Caniparoli, Val	1973
Andros, Gus	1948	Bintley, David (G.A.)	1994	Cappara, Michael	1970
Antisdel, Karen	1979	Black, Sherron	1975	Carlisle, Eldon	1951
Antonia, Ms.	1935	Blake, Jennifer	1992	Carlson, Deirdre	1972
Apple, Lisa	1989	Blanc, Nicolas	2003	Carlson, Gardner	1972
Arce, David	1999	Blanco, Clara	2001	Carlton, Janet	1939
Arkatov, Gloria	1939	Bliss, Barbara	1933	Carlyle, David	1937
Arkatov, Victoria	1939	Bliss, Olive	1947	Carmassi, Joseph	1943
Armos, Iris	1964	Block, Arnold/Arran/Yonkel	1935	Carmita (G.A.)	1935
Arnold, Bene	1949	Blum, Corinna	1998	Carpenter, Jan	1952
Arntz, Jo Ellen	1983	Boada, Joan (G.A. 1998)	1999	Carpenter, Melissa	1989
Arrona, Philippe	1969	Boatwright, Christopher	1986	Carr, Natalie/Natasha	1941
Arvola, Soili	1968	Bodine, Lori	1980	Carrabba, Marco	1983
Asonovich, Genevieve	1944	Bohm, Cecilia	1942	Carson, Shirley	1952
Asquith, Ruby	1940	Bolm, Adolph	1933	Carter, Francis	1955
Autrand, Claire	1945	Bonnefous, Jean-Pierre (G.A.)	1974	Carter, Richard	1952
Averty, Karin	1987	Booth, Velerie	1946	Cartt, Susan	1963
Avila, Ms.	1935	Borja, Claudia	1934	Carvajal, Carlos	1951
		Bortoluzzi, Paolo (G.A.)	1962/1976	Cassand, Rudolphe	1992
Bachich, Annette	1962	Boseman, Beverly	1943	Cassidy, Joan	1943
Badertscher, Barbara	1944	Bouchard, Madeleine	1973	Castilla, Antonio	1988
Baer, Johanna	1984	Bowen, Jane	1944	Cate, Nicholas	1973
Bailey, Francis	1939	Bradley, Carla	1934	Chadwick, Glen	1953
Bailey, Sally	1947	Bradley, Julie	1952	Champion, Marge (G.A.)	1976
Bain, Bruce	1960	Bradshaw, Isobel	1933	Chang, Stephanie (App.)	1990
Baker, Catherine	1998	Brady, Joan	1957	Chapman, Deidre	1992
Baker, Dale	1985	Bramer, Dalene	1997	Chappell, Gina	1942
Bakova, Pega	1936	Brandenhoff, Peter	1992/1998	Charisse, Nico	1933
a.k.a. Bates, Peggy		Brandner, Eildon	1935	Chetwood, Ronald	1937
Bancroft, Wallace	1933	Brannin, Jerome	1957	Chew, Sedley	1990
Barber, Lori	1998	Bratoff, Anatole	1934	Chisholm, Milton	1936
Barbour, Joan	1942	Bratoff, George	1933	Choi, Maureen	2000
Barth, Carmen	1980	Breedlove, Bill	1965	Christensen, Harold (G.A.)	1937
Basile, Andrea (App.)	1998	Brennan, Wayne	1955	Christensen, Lew (G.A.)	1937
Basuino, Alton	1948	Bright, Brantly	1972	Christensen, Willam	1937
Batcheller, Catherine	1982	Broderick, Maureen	1973	Chung, Frances	2001
Batchelor, Lorene	1953	Brody, Lori	1969	Cifuentes, Horacio	1979

1994

San Francisco Ballet presents the world premiere of Helgi Tomasson's full-length ballet *Romeo and Juliet*.

For the first time in its history, San Francisco Ballet performs at the Palais Garnier in Paris, presenting two mixed-repertory programs.

1995

San Francisco Ballet presents twelve ballet companies and twelve world premieres by choreographers during an unprecedented two weeks of creative exchange and collaboration. UNited We Dance: An International Festival commemorates the 50th anniversary of signing the United Nations Charter in 1945.

Michael Kane, San Francisco Ballet master carpenter, 1969 to 1995, is awarded the Lew Christensen Medal.

(App.) = Apprentice
(G.A.) = Guest Artist

	joined
Cisneros, Evelyn	1977
Clark, Alice	1936
Clark, Susan Barbara	1936
Clarke, Thatcher	1963
Clarkson, Courtney	2004
Clement, Janne	1976
Cline, J.	1933
Cochran, Warren	1947
Coffman, Vernon	1965
Cohn, Wilma	1944
Coler, Constance	1950
Coll, David	1966
Collins, Jeremy	1993
Coltron, Evelyn	1943
Coma Rosello, Blanca	1995
Connoly, Patricia	1933
Conroy, Pamela	1953
Converse, Payne	1940
Cook, Ms.	1935
Cooke, Allan	1933
Cooper, Duncan	1989
Cortaz, Joan	1942
Cosi, Liliana (G.A.)	1974
Cotton, Dorothy	1933
Cotton, Kester	1994
Courtney, Nigel	1979
Courtot de Bouteille, Bernard	1994
Coutereel, Steve	1996
Cowden, Laurie	1971/1981
Cox, Katherine	1981
Cragun, Richard (G.A.)	1974
Craig, E.	1934
Crawford, Jane	1933
Crethar, Jason	1993
Cristen, Grant	1937
Crocker, Virginia	1941
Crockett, Deane	1936
Crockett, Eric	1997
Crockett, Leslie	1975
Crowell, Ann	1949
Cruz, Diego	2006
Culbertson, Barbara	1959
Cummings, Celena	1939
Cuneo, Betty	1943
Cunningham, Genevieve	1933
Curry, Jere	1947
Curtez, Joan	1942
Curtis, James	1947
Dal Santo, Yvonne	1947
Dale, Anne	1972
D'amboise, Jacques (G.A.)	1960/1967
Damsgaard, Lars (App.)	1983
Danielian, Leon (G.A.)	1953/1959
Danilova, Alexandra (G.A.)	1952
Dano, Lazar	1967
Davey, Kimberly	1989
David, Mercedes (App.)	1983
Davis, Diana	1969
Davis, Jason	1994
De Garcia, Ralph	1934
De Graf, Anne	1936
De Heurtamont, Illiana	1966
De Lavallade, Carmen (G.A.)	1976
De Luce, Iris	1934
De Ruiz, Albert	1936

	joined
De Sosa, Emita	1937
De Vere, Joan	1964
De Vita, Marilyn	1950
De Witte, Odile	1971
Deane, Allyson	1966/1972
a.k.a. Segeler, Allyson	
Deivison, Daniel	2005
Del Lantis, Zoe	1939
Del Motte, Madeline	1937
Del Oro, Guillermo	1934
Delichtenberg, Marianne	1963
Delos, Donald	1953
Demmler, Nancy	1950
De Sola, Sasha (App.)	2006
Dettling, Aileen	1951
Devincenzi, Susan	1949
Di Giovanna, Joanna	1962
Diamond, Ms.	1939
Diana, Julie	1993
Diaz, Felipe	1993
Dickson, Nancy	1971/1978
Dimphel, Elva	1933
Dishong, Zola	1962
Dodge, Marcella	1943
Dodson, Betty Joan	1935
Doherty, Kathleen	1961
Dolin, Anton (G.A.)	1947
Domine, Eric	1941
Donald, Gemlyn	1964
Donne, Dieu	1937
Donohue, Leslie (App.)	1984
Doolin, Genevieve	1939
Douglas, Scott	1948
a.k.a. Hicks, Jimmy	
Dow, Simon	1985
Downing, Andrea	1939
Drayer, Cynthia	1985
Drew, Roderick	1954
Duclos, Lisa	1971
Duffus, Barrie	1967
Duggan, Leo	1949
Dunn, Elizabeth (App.)	1985
Dunn, Patricia	1948
Dunnigan, Joseph	1944
Dwyer, Michael	1973
Eames, Janet	1936
Eaton, Michael	1996
Echegaray, Nina	1988
Edgecumbe, Lodena (G.A.)	1937
Edgerton, Joan	1946
Edwards, Charles	1953
Eglevsky, André (G.A.)	1954
Elizabeth, Courtney	2003
Elliott, Patricia	1953
Ellison, Edward	1988
Ellison, Heidi	1973
Empey, Glenda	1953
Enders, Uta	1964
Engstrom, Jon	1966
Enman, Marion	1936
Erickson, Betsy	1964/1972
Eryck, Donald	1969
Escudero, Vicente (G.A.)	1935
Esquivel, Jorge	1993
Evans, Helen	1939

	joined
Fagundes, Christina	1983
Fames, Janet	1936
Faneuf	1942
Farr, Hayley	2004
Farrell, Suzanne (G.A.)	1976
Faulkner, Ralph	1936
Faulls, Branden	1997
Fealy, Dan	1936
Feijoo, Lorena	1999
Feinberg, Ronald	1950
Felsch, Joaquin	1942
Ferguson, Margaret	1933
Ferguson, Mildred	1939
Fernandez, Royes (G.A.)	1959
Ferrier, André (G.A.)	1944
Ficzere, Attila	1973
Filipov, Alexander	1974/1978
Finlay, Mary Barbara	1949
Fishel, Winifred	1935
Fitzell, Roy (G.A.)	1948
Fitzgerald, Marion	1933
Flandro, Ronnie	1943
Fletcher, Guy (App.)	2003
Flyzik, Irene	1933
Fnick, Virginia	1941
Foch, Nina (G.A.)	1964
Foley, Ann	1981
Fonteyn, Margot (G.A.)	1964
Ford, Katherine	1955
Foster, Sarah (App.)	1992
Fox, Tim	1986
Fraley, Ingrid	1968
France, Joe	1960
Francesca	1934
a.k.a. Guigni, Francesca; Ledova, Francesca; Romanoff, Francesca	
Franklin, Robert	1938
Freeman, Charles	1938
Freeman, Claire	1938
Frellson, Robert	1945
Frick, Pearl	1940
Frieder, Tally	1988
Fuerstner, Fiona	1950
Fujino, Koishi	1969
Fuller, Lee	1963
Fuqua, Max	1988
Fushille, Celia (App.)	1982
Gair, Joan	1972
Gale, Florence	1937
Gann, Rudolph	1938
Garcia Castilla, Jaime	2002
Garcia, Gonzalo	1998
Garde, Greta	1933
Garside, Martyn	2004
Garver, Dorothy	1935
Geary, Gladys	1939
Geipel, Robert	1951
Genshaft, Dana	2001
George, Carolyn	1948
Gerdes, Eileen	1986
Gerlach, Betty Jean	1937
Gerstner, Robert	1988
Gevurtz, Mattlyn	1937

	joined
Gibson, Diane	1963
Gibson, Elizabeth	1943
Gibson, Paul	1988
Gibson, Richard	1964
Gil, Jean-Charles	1986
Gilardi, Andrew	1943
Gillenwater, Carleton (App.)	1982
Girard, Aaron	1951
Gladstein, Robert	1960
Glimidakis, Anastasia (App.)	1980
Godkins, Paul	1936
Gold, Vera	1943
Golladay, Jeffrey	1998
Gomez, Cameron (App.)	1998
Gonzalez, Alexandra	1997
Gorbounoff, Gregory	1933
Gordon, Emmaleen	1936
Gordon, Susan	1984
Goshen, Harriet	1940
Grady, Claire	1936
Graham, Autumn	2004
Graham, Michael	1973
Grand, Nicole	2004
Greenley, Audrey	1944
Greenwood, Rachel	1994
Gregory, Cynthia (G.A. 1975)	1961
Grey, Jim	1949
Griffen, Tonia	1943
Griffin, Ikolo	1994
Guhlke, Antoinette	1944
Gyorfi, Victoria/Marilyn	1964/1971
Hall, George	1947
Halpin Ambuul, Emily	1999
Hamilton, Roberta	1950
Hammons, Suzanne	1959
Hampton, Thomas	1950
Hanf, Mary	1971
Hanlon, Scott	1970
Hanner, Thomas	1973
Hansen, Robert	1943
Hardie, David	1956
Hargraves, Lou Anne	1951
Harrington, Rex (G.A.)	1994
Harris, Donna	1960
Harshbarger, Joan	1953
Hart, Phillipp	1940
Hartley, Russell	1943
Harwest, Harry	1945
Hasstedt, Glen	1971
Hauser, Natalie	1993
Hay, William	1946
Haydee, Marcia (G.A.)	1974
Hayden, Melissa (G.A.)	1967
Hayes/Hays, Jeanne	1935
Hazinski, Michael	1980
Heft, Tiffany	1987
Heinemann, Kristine	1963
Helimets, Tiit	2005
Helms, Caroline	1953
Hench, Zachary	2000
Henderson, Helena	1942
Henderson, Howard	1958
Henderson, Melanie	1990
Herbert, Rebecca	1996
Herndon, Jerry	1958

	joined
Herr, Whitney (App.)	2002
Herrin, Julien	1956
Herst, Jeannde	1934
a.k.a. Taylor, Jeannde	
Hertzell, Edward	1948
Hevenor, Douglas	1970
Hicks, Janet	1944
Hildebrand, Carol	1953
Hill, Marjorie	1933
Hilliard, Riette	1933
Hines, Gregory (G.A.)	1982
Hink	1939
Hoagland, Helen	1934
Hobart, Jeffreys	1958
Hoctor, Daniel	1938
Hoffschneider, Lois	1937
Hohenstein, Rory	2000
Hoisington, Eric	1990
Holland, Thomas	1938
Holman, Nina	1953
Holmes, Eda	1980
Holt, Wendy	1966
Hooper, Corinne	1934
Hope, Kimberly (App.)	1990
Houser, Carolyn	1968
Houy, John	1968
Howard, Marlan	1952
Hseuh, Polly	1967
Hubbe, Nikolaj (G.A.)	1991
Hunter, Kathleen	1977
Huntress, Patricia	1954
Hutelin, Lynne	1971
Iglesias, Roberto	1949
Imaz, Elena	1942
Irwin, Jane	1958
Irwin, Robert	1938
Isham, Irene	1933
Ishikawa, Tokuko	1962
Ivory, Ashley	2002
Jacobs, Nancy	1945
Jacobsen, Marion	1942
Jacobson, Nancy	1943
James, Beverly	19xx
James, Evelyn	1933
James, Marie	1935
Jamison, Judith (G.A.)	1975
Janes, Howell	1943
Jarnac, Dorothy	1936
Jeppson, Pat	1955
Jhung, Finis	1961
Jiminez, Marie	1958
Johnson, Erika (G.A)	1997
Johnson, Juanita	1935
Johnson, Laura (App.)	1987
Johnson, Nancy	1944
Johnson, Virginia	1953
Johnson, Walter	1938
Johnson, William	1962
Jones, Cliff	1942
a.k.a. Jons, Kurt	
Jones, Kurt	1948
Jones, Stephanie	1975
Jordan, Yolanda	1992
Justin, David	1989

1997

The company tours to the prestigious Spoleto Festival U.S.A. and Hollywood Bowl, both for the first time, and returns to the Edinburgh International Festival.

While the War Memorial Opera House is closed for seismic renovations, San Francisco Ballet embarks on a multi-venue season, performing at the Center for the Performing Arts at Yerba Buena Gardens, the Palace of Fine Arts, and Zellerbach Hall at the University of California, Berkeley.

Denis de Couteau, music director and conductor, 1974 to 1998, and assistant conductor, 1968 to 1974, is awarded the Lew Christensen Medal.

San Francisco Ballet successfully completes Preserving a San Francisco Jewel, the most ambitious fundraising campaign in the company's history. $33 million financially secures the ballet, by building an endowment and providing operating funds while the company has been displaced from the Opera House.

(App.) = Apprentice
(G.A.) = Guest Artist

Name	joined
Kaiser, Adeline	2006
Kalimos, Leon	1947
Kalinin, Nika	1934
Karapetyan, Davit	2005
Karius, Jennifer	1988
Karl, Margaret	2002
Keever, Robert	1938
Kehlet, Niels (G.A.)	1973/1974
Keith, Hal	1942
Keith, Mimi	1983
Keith, Robert	1945
Kelly, Jane	1971
Kern, David	1981
Kersh, Henry	1964
Kessler, Dagmar (G.A.)	1974
Kessler, John	1953
Ketley, Alex	1994
Kiesov, Deborah	1971
Kimmerle, Milo	1937
Kitain, Michel (App.)	1977
Kitchens, Frank	1941
Kivitt, Ted (G.A.)	1976
Klakowicz, Roberta	1944
Klyce, Stacey (App.)	2000
Kneiper, Dorothy	1938
Kneiss, Gloria	1943
Knick, Virginia	1941
Knight, Pat	1960
Koerber, Betty	1949
Kogan, Ellen	1969
Kohn, Natalie	1981
Kolodin, Michael	1933
Koolish, Deborah	1967
Koovshinoff, Natasha	1944
Kostalki, Linda	1974
Kostich, Sonja	1992
Kostik, Jirjana	1969
Kotchik, Alice	1940
Krauklis, Vera	1937
Krauter, Marvin	1942
Krisman, Kim	1962
Kruse, Lois B.	1935
Kubes, Mary Alyce	1949
Kuranaga, Misa (App.)	2001
La Fetra, Jacqueline	1943
Lacarra, Lucia	1997
Lagios, Penelope	1966
Lang, Harold	1939
Lanham, Mark	1980
Larsen, Niels Bjorn (G. A.)	1994
Lauche, Clare	1933
Lauermann, Margaret	1969
Launspach, Roberta	1948
Laveau, Carolyn	1939
Lavelle, Rene	1934
Lavery, Leslie	1944
Lavery, Sean	1973
Lawler, Louise	1953
Lawler, Phyllis	1933
Le Crone, Arlend	1946
Leavitt, Gerard	1964
LeBlanc, Sherri	1995
LeBlanc, Tina	1992
Legate, Stephen	1991
Leitch, Patricia	1948
Lemus, Maurice	1958
Lennard, Paul	1941
Leporsky, Zoya	1938
a.k.a. Liporska, Zoya	
Leroy, Pascale	1986
Levy, Ruth	1937
Lewis, Curt Conner	1933
Lewitzke, Alice LuAn	1997
Liashenko, Ludmilla	1949
Lilly, Shannon	1986
Lind, P.	1934
Lintz, Hope	1939
Lintz, Mark	1942
Lipitz, Kenneth	1966
Lippi, Tosca	1939
Little, Vivian	1978
Lloyds, Margaret	1947
Long, Kristin	1990
Long, Virginia	1991/1993
Longtin, Ann Marie	1965
Looper, Ted	1960
Lopez, Antonio	1979
Lopez, Marisa	1994
Lopuknova, Ludmila	1985
Lordon, Daniel	1971
Lorraine, Serrita	1936
Loscavio, Elizabeth	1986
Loswick, Sonia	1944
Louis, Robert	1952
Loungway, Stuart	1992
Low, Megan	1997
Lowell, Ellen	1936
Loyd, Sue	1956
Loyola, Caroline	1998
Ludlow, Conrad (G.A. 1967)	1953
Luthi, Alice/Alys	1933
Lydon, Katherine	1991
Lynn, Mari	1940
Lyon, James	1958
Mac Ritchie, Norman	1950
Macejunas, Deborah	1970
Madia, Georgio	1990
Madsden, Dagmar	1953
Maduell, Grace	1983
Maffre, Muriel	1990
Magierek, Pauli	1998
Magno, Susan	1975
Maier, Tracy-Kai	1980/1985
Maijala, Devani	1994
Makarova, Natalia (G.A.)	1974
Malek, Brian	2006
Mallozzi, John	1953
Malm, Shirley	1933
Mamales, George	1954
Mancato, Rafael	1936
Mandradjieff, Lindy	1997
Manero, Jose	1945
Mangosing, Jonathan	2002
Mann, Grace	1941
Manners, Joseph	1945
Manning, Joyce	1939
Mansfeldt, Irene	1945
Marasco, Frank	1938
Marische, Louise	1933
Markova, Alicia (G.A.)	1947
Marks, Diana	1966
Marlow, Pamela	1958
Marshall, Dennis	1976/1981
Martin, Barbarajean	1969
Martin, Jacqueline	1937
Martin, Jose	1995
Martin, Keith	1975
Martin, Moises	1999
Martin, Ruben	2000
Martins, Peter (G.A.)	1976
Martuza, Kathleen	1997
Marvin, Ronald	1940
Marx, Linda	1970
Mascagno, Ernest	1938
Mathis, Lorin	2000
Matthews, C.	1934
Matthews, Laurence	1969
Maule, Sara	1968
Mayes, Lucille	1933
Maynard, Parrish	1998
McBride, Patricia (G.A.)	1974
McConnell, Billy	1933
McCoy, L. Harlan	1944
McCullagh, Alexandra	2006
McDonnell, Diane	1953
McFall, John	1965/1971
McGinnis, Andrea	2005
McIntyre, Barbara	1939
McLaughlin, Gaby	1933
McLaughlin, Margaret	1972
McLeod, Richard	1994
McMillan, Justin	1995
McMillan, Lois	1935
McNaughton, David	1976/1983
McNulty, Erin	2000
Mednick, Joanna	2001
Mehrkins, Ms.	1935
Meistrell, Diana	1977
Meja, Daniel	1984
Meyer, Lynda	1963
Meyer-Lorey, Alexandra	2004
Meyer, Roberta	1950
Meyers, Cynthia	1971
Miller, Eduardo	1951
Miller, Jonathan	1979
Miller, Sharon Lee	1944
Miner, Elizabeth	1997
Mitchell, Kathleen	1983
Mitoff, Janice	1948
Molat, Pascal	2002
Mondonville, J.G.	1935
Mondoux, Christopher (App.)	2006
Montaner, Julian	1983
Montaner, Linda	1980
Moore, Augusta	1982
Moore, Brooke Taylor	1999
Moore, Gary	1972
Moorhead, Kristi	1972
Moran, Consuelo	1969
Moran, Eccleston	1933
Morey, Norman	1956
Morey, Zelda	1937
a.k.a. Nerina/Norina, Zelda	
Morgan, Victoria	1979
Moroshita, Yoko (G.A.)	1977
Mortimer, Zelda	1936
Moser, Molly	1936
Mourelatos, John	1978
Mraz, Fiala	1943
Munier, Elaine	1997
Murphy, Russell	1980
Musante, Muriel	1933
Nabeshina, Irene	1951
Nachtsheim, Gigi	1968
Nahser, Heather	1990
Nari, Mr.	1935
Nassie, Georgia	1943
Nathanson, Judy	1945
Nedviguine, Guennadi	1997
Neilsen, Norma	1938
Nelson, Frank	1941
a.k.a. Nelson, Peter	
Nelson, Marcus	1947
Nelson, Mark	1942
Nelson, Ted	1941
Nelson, Ted	1970
Ness, Anton	1972
Ness, Gina	1972
Newer, Dorothy	1938
Nielsen, Diana	1959
Nissinen, Mikko	1987
Noble, Edwina	1942
Noe, Susan	1935
Norlander, Sven	1968
Norman, Patricia	1963
Norman, Steven	1995
Norton, Janyce	1937
Noyes, Betina	1937
Nureyev, Rudolf (G.A.)	1964
Nuyts, Jan	1977
Nzerem, Chidozie	1996
Odhner, Ellen	1944
Ogilvie, Richard	1972
Ohman, Frank	1959
Okamura, Kimberley	1988
Oliva, Mary Alice	1951
Oliver, Edward	1935
Olson, Mariellen	2002
Ordway, Frank	1963
O'Rourke, Kevin	1969
Orr, Terry	1959
Orza, Aaron	2000
Ostaggi, Elizabeth	1951
Otis, Billie/Willa	1937
Oukrainsky, Serge	1937
Pace, Loraine	1940
Paciotti, Anita	1968
Palmer, David	1994
Panaieff, Michel (G.A.)	1943
Panella, Holly	1994
Panov, Galina (G.A.)	1975/1976
Panov, Valery (G.A.)	1975/1976
Parades, Betty	1939
Parades, Nemesio	1940
Parello, Leila	1970
Parin, Andrew	1933
Parker, Barton II	1987
Parker, James	1940
Parker, Margo	1947
Parker, Mary	1951
Parker, Suzanne	1933
Parungao, Magdalene	1984
Pascal, Claire	2005
Patterson, John	1966
Patterson, Ralph	1944
Patzelt, Lydia	1933
Paul, Henry	1940
Paul, Virginia	1940
Paulini, Philippa	1933
Pausch, Adea	1953
Paxman, Gordon	1951
Peary, Kristine	1981
Pech, Lawrence	1986
Pelzer, Vantania	1982
Penrod, Jim	1958
Perego, Marguerite	1943
Peregrine, David	1984
Perez, Patricia	2006
Perkins, Cosette	1937
Perri, Ms.	1935
Perry, Joy	1953
Pesina, Victor	1980
Peter, Zoltan	1978
Peterson, Kirk	1981
Peterson, Marianne	1944
Petrillo, Rosemary	1958
Petro, Rudolph	1933
Petrusich, John	1937
Pfeil, Roberta	1973
Phegan, Maria	1994
Phillips, Joseph	2004
Piantino, Pablo	1999
Pierce, Benjamin (G.A. 1995–1996)	1997
Pierre, Cyril	1996
Pineda, Carlos	1933
Piner, Bruce (App.)	1976
Pipit-Suksun, Nutnaree	2004
Plain, Mikhael	1996
Plato, Ms.	1935
Poindexter, Ron	1963
Polinski, Betty	1942
Pons, Denise	1980
Poole, Virginia	1943
Possokhov, Yuri	1994
Post, Janet	1947
Post, Laura	1935
Poston, Eileen	1933
Powell, Marilyn	1944
Prager, Patricia	1959
Price, Deborah	1971
Pring, George	1933
Prosch, Rosalie	1939
Prud'homme, Kay	1973
Pulford, Marti	1969
Queen, Clyde	1955
Quick, Cynthia	1968
Rabu, Renald	1969
Radding, Celene	1936
Raisbeck, Virginia	1935
Raisch, Leila	1934
Ramaciotti, Julio	1933
Ramey, Valla	1943

1998

The company returns home to the War Memorial Opera House, after completion of a two-year seismic renovation, in time to celebrate its 65th Anniversary Season.

San Francisco Ballet presents the West Coast premiere of Lar Lubovitch's full-length ballet *Othello* (a co-commission with American Ballet Theatre).

1999

San Francisco Ballet presents the world premiere of Helgi Tomasson's full-length ballet *Giselle*.

Chris Hellman, board of trustees chair, 1991 to 1999, and board member since 1983, is awarded the Lew Christensen Medal.

2000

San Francisco Ballet presents six world premieres in two programs over one week for the inaugural Discovery Program. The program includes premieres from four San Francisco Ballet Principal Dancers: Julia Adam, David Palmer, Yuri Possokhov, and Christopher Stowell.

Name	joined
Ramos, David	1969
Randall, Julia	1938
Randazzo, Anthony	1987
Raub, Marcianne	1944
Rayburn, Nada	1938
Redick, Jared	1991
Reed, Janet	1937
Reese, Doral	1947
Reikman, Ruth	1939
Reiman, Elise	1933
Renov, Ramon	1933
Retle, Jean	1958
Reyburn, Josephine	1940
Reyes, Andre	1981
Reyes, Benjamin	1967
Reyes, Genie	1949
Reynolds, Brooke	2000
Rhoads, Julie (App.)	1989
Richardson, Desmond (G.A)	1998
Richardson, Dolores	1946
Richie, Joyce	1939
Richter, Gertrude	1934
Riedel, Jymmi	1943
Riggins, Earl	1938
Rios, Mauricio	1949
Ritter, Laurie	1975
Roberts, Shannon	2005
Robinson, Christine	1958
Robinson, Nancy	1961
Roche, Aurora	1936
Rogers, Lily	2005
Rogers, Margaret	1933
Romanoff, Dimitri	1933
Roof, Leone	1935
Rosenburg, Ronald	1973
Rosenheim, Gail	1985
Ross, Ms.	1939
Ross, Ron	1953
Rosso, Ralph	1947
Rothwell, Maureen	1971
Rothwell, R. Clinton	1965
Rowan, Miriam	2004
Rowland, Deanne	1965
Rubino, Michael	1963
Rudnick, Lia	1969
Rufer, Rachel	1998
Ruiz, Alex	1952
Ruiz, Maclovia	1933
Ruiz, Marie	1933
Russ, Virginia	1933
Russell, Gregory	1984
Russell, Patrick	1983
Russell, Paul	1980
Ruud, Tomm (G.A. 1971)	1975
Rykin, Roman	1996
Sachs, L.	1934
Sage, Russell	1953
Sakajian	1942
Sakowsky, Juliana	1964
Salano (G.A.)	1945
Salazar, Constance	1937
Sanders, Tom	1963
Sansom, Bruce (G.A.)	1991/1992
Santos, Danielle	2005
Santos, Tina	1973
Sassoon, Janet	1944
Schaefer, Karen (App.)	1976
Schaeffer, Keith	1983
Schaufuss, Peter (G.A.)	1974
Schiller, Jean	1951
Schofield, Tiekka	2001
Schorer, Suki	1956
Schroeder, Royal B.	1933
Schroeter, Ruth	1935
Schueler, Ruth Louise	1933
Schull, Amanda	2000
Schulte, Ms.	1935
Schwennesen, Don	1976
Scott, Shelley	1986
Scribner, Garen	2004
Self, Christina	1985
Sellman, Bernice	1933
Semochenko, Irene	1933
Sessions, Sara	1989
Shaeffer, Rosalind	1936
Shapiro, Muriel	1953
Sharp, Christie	1961
Sharpe, Richard	1945
Sheeren, Susan	1971
Shepard, Ada	1960
Shepard, Kay	1935
Shiga, Misae (G.A.)	1997
Shimonauff, Alexis	1933
Shockley, Jonathan	1999
Shore, Sharon	1944
Shwab, Fred	1955
Sikes, Richard	1971
Silva, Rodolfo	1943
Silver, Mark	1982
Simmons, Daniel	1970
Simoneau, Maurine	1958
Simpson, Konrad	1997
Siprelle, Richard	1934
Skinner, Patricia	1943
Slater, Josephine	1936
Slayen, Leah (App.)	1997
Slazer, Constance	1937
Smart, Eldon	1951
Smith, Belva	1953
Smith, Charles	1936
Smith, Damian	1996
Smith, Duncan	1942
Smith, Nicki	1971
Smith, Salicia	1965
Smolen, Molly	2006
Smuin, Michael	1957
Snider, Sharon	1946
Snodgrass, Ernest	1933
Snyder, Alice	1933
Snyder, Evelyn	1933
Sofranko, James	2000
Sohm, Jim	1975/1985
Solomakha, Vadim	1995
Sorkin, Naomi	1973
Sorvo, Salli	1947
Spassoff, Bojan	1973
Spaulding, Anthony	2006
Spottswood, Donald	1947
Sprading, Marc	1985
Stackpole, Dana	1990
Stahl, Jennifer	2006
Stalley, Suzanne	1961
Stanton, Jeff	1990
Stanton, Thomas	1971
Stapleton, Virginia	1961
Starbuck, James	1934
Starbuck, Nicole	1995
Staver, Frederick	1938
Stephans, Marsha	1975
Stepick, Wanda	1945
Sterba, Natalie	1977
Stewart, Benjamin	2006
Stewart, Lee	1952
Stewart, Matthew	2003
Stoddard, Jud	1966
Stoney, Wiora	1937
Storey, Edward	1943
Storm, Carol	1970
Story, Molly (App.)	1985
Stowell, Christopher	1985
Stowell, Kent	1957
Streeter, Patricia	1957
Sturges, Lee	1933
Sugano, Mayo	2000
Sullivan, John	1969
Suminsby, Barbara	1940
Sund, Robert	1978
Swift, Akisa	1992
Swift, Peggy	1940
Swift, Virginia	1941
Swing, Roberta	1962
Sykes, Richard	1970
Sylvester, Patricia	1971
Syndon, Ruth	1935
Tallchief, Maria (G.A.)	1954/1960
Tamon, Arnold	1936
Tan, Yuan Yuan	1995
Taylor, Peter	1986
Tedesco, Emily (App.)	2002
Thatcher, Ian	1990
Thomas, Geoffrey	1970
Thomas, Michael	1973
Thomas, Ms. L.	1935
Thompson, Jim	1989
Thompson, Norman	1939
Thompson, Ralph	1936
Thorson, Robert	1943
Tienken, Elizabeth	1973
Tikannen, Matti (G.A.)	1970
Tjomsland, Eloise	1964
Toepleman, Edward	1947
Tomlinson, Nadine	1973
Tompkins, Beatrice	1943
Topciy, Alexander	1979
Torrado, Sergio	1999
Toscano, Synde	1933
Toumanova, Tamara (G.A.)	1948
Tracy, Paula	1957/1973
Treadwell, Lois	1942
Treen, Virginia	1934
Tribble, Patricia	1951
True, Sallie	1972
Tucker, Jeannette	1939
Tucker, Robert	1943
Tully, Michael	1970
Tumkovsky, Timothy	1972
Turetzky, Michele	1972
Turner, Margaret	1933
Uptegrove, Richard	1971
Valdez, Arnoldo	1935
Van Alstyne, Alexander	1989
Van Der Kamp, Walter	1933
Van Dyck, Wendy	1979
Van Horn, Eugenia	1957
Van Patten, Dolores	1935
Van Patten, Sarah	2002
Van Sickle, Brett (App.)	2002
Van Winkle, Rick	1970
Var, Danya	1933
Varjan, Stephan	1972
Vasilaky, Katya	1997
Vasilieff, Nicolai	1933
Vazquez, Geraldine	1948
Vazquez, Roland	1947
Verchinina, Nina (G.A.)	1938
Verdy, Violette (G.A.)	1970/1971/1972
Vesselofzorov, Roman	1933
Vest, Vane	1972
Vickers, Joan	1943
Vickrey, Robert	1961
Vilanoba, Pierre-François	1998
Villanueva, Josepha	1967
Villella, Edward (G.A.)	1972
Viselli, Rachel	1999
Visentin, Gail	1960
Vitale, Adriano (G.A.)	1959
Vollmar, Jocelyn	1939
Wagner, Erik	1995/1997
Wahl, Gary	1973
Waldo, Katita	1988
Walker, Amanda	1988
Walker, Dorothy	1935
Walker, Laura	1973
Wallace, Mimi	1960
Warner, Catherine	1968
Warner, Katherine	1980
Warner, Robert (App.)	1977
Warren, Larry	1958
Warwick, Alyan	1937
Watson, Leah	1993
Watson, Megan	1993
Watts, Melanie (App.)	1985
Waxman, Gina	1959
Weber, Bill	1941
Weber, Diana	1973
Weber, Sam (G.A.)	1972
Weber, Tony	1958
Weber, William	1942
Weichardt, Eric	1976
Weingarten, Judy	1971
Weisbarth, Bonnie	1971
Weiss, Jerome	1973
Wendorf, Vernon	1948
Wenger, Evelyn	1933
Wennerholm, Wana	1938
West, Golden	1935
Westlake, Rachel (App.)	1979
Whalen, Sally	1943
Wharton, Quinn	2005
Wheater, Ashley	1989
Whistler, Doris	1940
White, Gabrilla	1937
White, John	1996
White, Josephine	1936
White, Onna/Anna	1938
White, Shari	1960
Whited, Ms. E.	1935
Whitney, Margaret	1936
Whitson, Eileen	1949
Wickman, Wendy (App.)	1980
Wieman, Virginia	1935
Williams, Caroline	1944
Williams, Christina	1970
Williams, Kerry	1966
Williams, Merle	1937
Williams, Susan	1970
Williams, Wana	1942
Wilson, Bobbie	1940
Wilson, Jennifer (App.)	1988
Wilson, June	1944
Wilson, Marjorie	1936
Wilson, Michelle	1992/1997
Winfield, John	1998
Wing, Lita/Lyda	1935
Winters, Dan	1957
Wiseman, Maureen/Anne	1965
Witt, Diana	1951
Wojtwicz, Karen (App.)	2000
Wolf, Stephanie	1973
Wolfram, Eric	1992
Wollenberg, M.	1934
Wong, Daniel (App.)	1986
Wood, Barbara	1937
Woods, Deane	1943
Woods, Robert (App.)	1973
Woodworth, Julia	1935
Wright, Courtney	2000
Wright, Gabriella	1937
Wu, Ming-Hai	1990
Wynn, Billy	1953
Yamamoto, Hansuke	2001
Yazolino, Felice	1934
Young, Eleanor	1935
Young, Leslie	1986
Younger, Judith	1951
Zahorian, Vanessa	1997
Zaretskiy, Kirill	2001
Zdobinski, Deborah	1974
Zegarelli, Carmela	1979
Zelensky, Igor (G.A.)	1996
Zhukov, Yuri	1989
Ziehr, Jean	1942
Zimmerman, Jamie	1977
Zinoun, Jais	1989/1993
Zonn, Eugenia	1934
Zubiria, Alexi	1986

181

2001

San Francisco Ballet tours to London for its first engagement at the Royal Opera House, Covent Garden.

Music Director Denis de Coteau passes away.

San Francisco Ballet engages in a unique cultural exchange with Paris Opéra Ballet. San Francisco Ballet presents the company in Rudolf Nureyev's *La Bayadère* and Angelin Preljocaj's *Le Parc* in Paris Opera Ballet's historic San Francisco debut.

San Francisco Ballet tours to Santander, Spain, and then on to Paris to perform at the Palais Garnier for the first time since 1994. While in Paris, Artistic Director Helgi Tomasson is awarded the rank of *Officier* in the prestigious French Order of Arts and Letters.

Willam Christensen, former San Francisco Ballet choreographer, ballet master, and artistic director, dies in Salt Lake City at age 99.

75th Anniversary Celebration Committee

Honorary Chairs

Chris Hellman
Lucy Jewett

Co-Chairs

Mary B. Cranston
J. Stuart Francis
Margaret G. Gill

Events Subcommittee Co-Chairs

Ann and Robert Fisher
Mary Jo and Richard Kovacevich
Carl F. and Yurie Pascarella

Funding Subcommittee Chair

John S. Osterweis

History Subcommittee Co-Chairs

Kristen A. Avansino
Susan A. Van Wagner

Public Relations Subcommittee Chair

Mary B. Cranston

School & Education Subcommittee Co-Chairs

Wendy Wasson Bingham
Melinda B. Pressler

Jola Anderson
Deborah Bocci
Susan S. Briggs
Jennifer Caldwell
Beth F. Cobert
Paula Elmore
Jacqueline L. Erdman
Sonia H. Evers
Erin Glenn
Mrs. John P. Grotts
Jeffrey P. Hays, M.D.
Christina E. A. Hecht
Libby Heimark
James H. Herbert, II
Donald F. Houghton
Pamela J. Joyner
Jean Larette
James J. Ludwig
Dr. Katalin Kadar Lynn
Marissa Mayer
Jennifer J. McCall
Stephanie B. Russell
Christine Russell
O.J. Shansby
Christine E. Sherry
Charlotte Mailliard Shultz
Fran A. Streets
Judy C. Swanson
Patricia A. TeRoller
Tracey B. Warson
Paul L. Wattis, III
Wayne Woodruff
Stephen A. Zellerbach

Great Benefactors

In celebration of its 75th Anniversary, the Company honors each of the following donors, whose cumulative giving to San Francisco Ballet is $1 million or more, as a Great Benefactor of America's first professional ballet company.

AT&T
Bank of America Foundation
The State of California
California Arts Council
Estate of Lewis and Emily Callaghan
Mrs. Daniel H. Case III
Chevron Corporation
Deloitte
Rudolph W. Driscoll
First Republic Bank
Ford Foundation
Diana Stark and J. Stuart Francis
Estate of George L. Frierson
Stephen and Margaret Gill Family Foundation
Richard & Rhoda Goldman Fund
Grants for the Arts
Colleen and Robert D. Haas
Evelyn & Walter Haas, Jr. Fund
Mimi and Peter Haas
Miriam and Peter Haas Fund
Walter & Elise Haas Fund
Estate of Katharine Hanrahan
William Randolph Hearst Foundation
Chris and Warren Hellman
The Herbert Family
William and Flora Hewlett Foundation
The Edward E. Hills Fund
Estate of Dora Donner Ide
James Irvine Foundation
George F. Jewett, Jr. 1965 Trust
Estate of Mildred Johnson
Mrs. Gorham B. Knowles
Koret Foundation
Catherine and Paul Lego
Mrs. Edmund W. Littlefield
The Marver Family
Andrew W. Mellon Foundation
National Endowment for the Arts
Bernard Osher Foundation
John Osterweis and Barbara Ravizza
Yurie and Carl Pascarella
The Thomas J. and Gerd Perkins Foundation
Kenneth Rainin
Mr. George R. Roberts
Bob Ross
Gordon Russell
San Francisco Ballet Auxiliary
San Francisco Foundation
Kathleen Scutchfield
Shubert Foundation, Inc.
The Smelick Family
The Swanson Foundation
Mr. Richard J. Thalheimer
Visa USA
Phyllis C. Wattis
Wells Fargo
E.L. Wiegand Foundation
Diane B. Wilsey
Akiko Yamazaki and Jerry Yang

San Francisco Ballet Association

† Past Chair
*ex officio

Board of Trustees

James H. Herbert, II
Co-chair of the Board and Executive Committee

Pamela J. Joyner
Co-chair of the Board and Executive Committee

Chris Hellman†
Chair Emeritus

J. Stuart Francis†
Vice Chair

Lucy Jewett
Vice Chair

Paul G. Lego
Vice Chair

James D. Marver
Vice Chair

Robert M. Smelick
Vice Chair

Diane B. Wilsey
Vice Chair

Richard C. Barker
Treasurer

Jennifer J. McCall
Secretary

Susan S. Briggs
Assistant Secretary

Helgi Tomasson
Artistic Director

Glenn McCoy*
Executive Director

Michael C. Abramson
David L. Anderson
Jola Anderson
Kristen A. Avansino
Wendy Wasson Bingham
Deborah Bocci
Marjorie Burnett
Jennifer Caldwell
Beth F. Cobert
Michael G. Conn
Mary B. Cranston
William G. Duck
Stephanie Ejabat
Jacqueline L. Erdman
Sonia H. Evers
Irwin Federman
Ann C. Fisher
Margaret G. Gill
Richard N. Goldman
Sally Hambrecht
Jeffrey P. Hays, MD
Libby Heimark
Ingrid von Mangoldt Hills
Hank J. Holland
Thomas E. Horn
Donald F. Houghton
Christopher P. Johns
Mary Jo Kovacevich
Marissa Mayer
Kenneth P. McNeely
Alexander R. Mehran
Byron R. Meyer
James E. Milligan
John S. Osterweis
Carl F. Pascarella
Melinda B. Pressler
George R. Roberts
Claude N. Rosenberg Jr.
Christine Russell
O.J. Shansby
Christine E. Sherry
Charlotte Mailliard Shultz
David Stanton
Fran A. Streets
Judy C. Swanson
Patricia A. TeRoller
Richard J. Thalheimer
Susan A. Van Wagner
Lonna Wais
Tracey B. Warson
Paul L. Wattis, III
Timothy C. Wu
Akiko Yamazaki
Janice Hansen Zakin, MD

Trustees Emeriti

Thomas W. Allen
Charles Dishman
Garrettson Dulin Jr. †
Mrs. Lawrence D. Dunham
Neil E. Harlan†
George B. James†
David A. Kaplan
Mrs. Gorham B. Knowles
James J. Ludwig†
Nancy H. Mohr
Gerald E. Napier
Thomas J. Perkins
Marie-Louise Pratt
Kenneth Rainin
George W. Rowe
Kathleen Scutchfield
L. Jay Tenenbaum
Dennis Wu
Stephen A. Zellerbach†

Associate Trustees

Mrs. John P. Grotts
President, SF Ballet Auxiliary

Christina E.A. Hecht
President, BRAVO

Stephanie B. Russell
President, ENCORE!

San Francisco Ballet Endowment Foundation Board of Directors

John S. Osterweis
President

George W. Rowe
Vice President

Thomas E. Horn
Treasurer

Patricia A. TeRoller
Secretary

Richard C. Barker
Susan S. Briggs
J. Stuart Francis
Chris Hellman
George B. James
James D. Marver
Carole Obley
Robert M. Smelick

2002

San Francisco Ballet returns to New York's City Center for the first time in four years.

The Juilliard School's Board of Trustees confers an honorary doctoral degree upon Helgi Tomasson.

San Francisco Ballet begins the first of a two-phase process to update and improve its building to better accommodate the needs of the growing organization.

2003

San Francisco Ballet presents the world premiere of the full-length ballet *Don Quixote*, co-choreographed by Artistic Director Helgi Tomasson and Principal Dancer Yuri Possokhov.

The company performs a program of works by Christopher Wheeldon at the Edinburgh International Festival.

Jocelyn Vollmar, former San Francisco Ballet dancer and San Francisco Ballet School faculty member, is awarded the Lew Christensen Medal.

San Francisco Ballet Association (continued)

San Francisco Ballet Board of Trustees

Leadership

Wallace M. Alexander President, SF Opera Association	1933, 1935–1936
Mrs. Stanley Powell Chairman, SF Opera Women's Committee	1933, 1935
No list available	1934
Robert W. Miller President, SF Opera Association	1937–1939, 1941
No list available	1940
Mrs. Julliard McDonald President, Ballet Guild	1942–1945, 1947, 1949
George Washington Baker President, Civic Ballet Association	1947
No list available	1948
No list available	1950
No list available	1951
Mrs. James Bodrero President, Ballet Guild	1952–1954
Mrs. William Bayless President, Ballet Guild	1955–1960
James J. Ludwig President, Ballet Guild	1961–1968
Derk R. TeRoller President, Ballet Guild	1968–1971
Stephen A. Zellerbach President, Ballet Association Chair, Ballet Association	1972–1973 1974
Mrs. G. W. Douglas Carver President, Ballet Association	1974
Garrettson Dulin Jr. Chair, Ballet Association	1975–1977
Philip S. Schlein Chair, Ballet Association	1978–1982
Neil E. Harlan Chair, Ballet Association	1983–1985
George B. James Chair, Ballet Association	1986–1991
Chris Hellman Chair, Ballet Association Chair Emeritus	1992–1999 2000–2007
J. Stuart Francis Chair, Ballet Association	2000–2002
James H. Herbert II Chair, Ballet Association Co-chair, Ballet Association	2003–2005 2006–present
Pamela J. Joyner Co-chair, Ballet Association	2006–present

San Francisco Ballet Auxiliary

Leadership

Lucinda Crocker	1972–1973
Jane Flahaven	1973–1974
Jerry Farber	1974–1975
Polly Duxbury	1975–1976
Vicki Fleishacker	1976–1977
Lynn McGowin	1977–1978
Jola Anderson	1978–1979
Millicent Dunham	1979–1980
Mary Falk	1980–1981
Marie Louise Pratt	1981–1982
Ann Schindler	1982–1983
Nancy Mohr	1983–1984
Manuela Broderick	1984–1985
P.J. Handeland	1985–1986
Ingrid Weiss	1986–1987
Caroline Brownstone	1987–1988
Dixie Furlong	1988–1989
Carlene Reininga	1989–1990
Janet Grosser	1990–1991
Jan Rogers and Lynne Baer	1991–1992
Lynne Baer	1992–1993
Carole Obley	1993–1995
Connie Harvey	1995–1997
Deborah Bocci	1997–1999
Judy Hobbs	1999–2001
Sandy Mandel	2001–2003
Elisabeth Petkevich	2003–2005
Lisa Grotts	2005–2007

San Francisco Ballet BRAVO

Leadership

Shirley LaMere	1981–1982
Elizabeth Meyer	1982–1984
Gordon Minton	1984–1985
Chauncey J. Smith	1985–1986
Cheryle Eymil	1986–1988
Judith Robertson	1988–1989
Chauncey J. Smith	1989–1990
Rudy Picarelli	1990–1993
Giovanna Jackson	1993–1994
Rudy Picarelli	1994–1995
Frances Eubanks	1995–1996
Rudy Picarelli	1996–1998
Betsy McGuigan	1998–1999
Wayne Woodruff	1999–2003
Gil Jewell	2003–2006
Christina E.A. Hecht	2006–2007

San Francisco Ballet ENCORE!

Leadership

Elizabeth Kramer (Founding President)	1993–1996
Carol Benz	1996–1998
Patrick Barber	1998–2000
Victoria Schreiber	2000–2002
Anne-Marie Fowler	2002–2004
Stephanie B. Russell	2004–2007

San Francisco Ballet Executive Directors

Leadership

Richard E. LeBlond Jr. President	1975–1987
Garrettson Dulin Jr. President	1987–1988
W. McNeil Lowry President	1988–1991
Joyce A. Moffatt Executive Director	1991–1993
Arthur Jacobus Executive Director	1993–2002
Glenn McCoy Executive Director	2002–present

2004

San Francisco Ballet is the first American ballet company to present the full-length ballet *Sylvia* with all-new choreography by Mark Morris.

Renovation is completed on the Ballet building. Improvements include a new Dancer Wellness Center, additional and improved studio space and locker rooms for dancers and students, and a five-story annex for administrative offices.

Lucy Jewett, long-term board member, is awarded the Lew Christensen Medal.

The company premieres a new *Nutcracker* production with original choreography by Helgi Tomasson, scenery and costumes by Tony Award winners Michael Yeargan and Martin Pakledinaz, and lighting by James F. Ingalls. The new production is the fifth in the company's history.

San Francisco Ballet Association (continued)

Board of Trustees

Members

San Francisco Opera Association, 1933–1941 +

Wallace M. Alexander
Frank B. Anderson
Charles R. Blyth
Arthur M. Brown, Jr.
George T. Cameron
Horace B. Clifton
Peter Conley
William W. Crocker
Milton H. Esberg
Mortimer Fleishhacker
Timothy Healy
Robert W. Miller
Edward F. Moffat
John Francis Neylan
Mrs. Stanley Powell
Richard M. Tobin
Nion R. Tucker

San Francisco Opera Women's Committee, 1933–1937 +

Mrs. H. B. Clifton
Marie Hicks Davidson
Mrs. William Fitzhugh
Mrs. Marcus S. Koshland
Mrs. Roger Lapham
Mrs. Stine Leis
Miss Edith Livermore
Sallie Maynard
Mrs. M.C. Porter
Mrs. Stanley Powell
Mrs. M. C. Sloss
Mrs. Sigmund Stern

San Francisco Ballet Guild, 1942–1971 †

Alex Anderson
Cal Anderson
Mrs. Wood Armsby
George Washington Baker
Mrs. George W. Baker
Francis Bascom
Alta A. M. Bates
Mrs. William Bayless
Nancy Bechtle
Mrs. James Bodrero
Mrs. Henry Brigham
Mrs. William W. Budge
Mrs. G. W. Douglas Carver
William Chester
Mrs. Drew Chidester
Harold Christensen
Lew Christensen
Willam Christensen
Charles H. Clifford
George D. Cohn
Mrs. Lammot Copeland Jr.
Mrs. Alfred Crapsey
Mrs. Sherman Crary
Mrs. Charles Crocker
Tracy Cummings
Mrs. Gardner A. Dailey
Mrs. Edward Daly
Roger Deas
Bruce Dohrmann
R. Stanley Dollar Jr.
Mrs. Allen Downing
Rudolph W. Driscoll
Joseph H. Dyer Jr.
Mrs. Warren G. Epstein
Milton H. Esberg Jr.
Trirey Ford
Edward Gauer
Virginia Gerould
Mrs. Ralph P. Gomez
Carl Ludwig Hansen
Mrs. Raymond E. Harroun
Alex Hart
Robert Haynie
Mrs. Randolph A. Hearst
Mrs. Frederick J. Hellman
Mrs. Louis E. Hendricks
Mrs. Hobart Hicks
Osgood Hooker
Mrs. Robert Howard
Mrs. Thomas Carr Howe Jr.
Mrs. Reed Hunt
John B. Huntington
Mrs. Covington Janin
Lucy Jewett
Mrs. Donald Johnston
Leon G. Kalimos
Chili Kohlenberg
Mrs. Marcus Koshland
Mrs. Roger Lapham Jr.
Daniel H. Lewis
Mrs. Davies Lewis
Mrs. Clarence Lindner
Larence Livingston

James J. Ludwig
Edmund B. MacDonald
Cyril Magnin
Mrs. Donald Magnin
Mrs. Grover Magnin
Mr. Leonard Martin
Mrs. Alexander B. McAllister
Grace Kennan McClatchy
Mrs. Julliard McDonald
J. Fenton McKenna, MD
Theodore Meyer
William A. Meyer
Mrs. Reyer Nixon
Mrs. Edgar Osgood
William Craighton Peet
Mrs. Hugh David Phillips
Robert Phillips Jr.
Mrs. George Pope Jr.
Mrs. Ashton Potter
Walter Prendergast
Mrs. Spelman Prentice
Mrs. Carey Ramey
John Redington
Leonard J. T. Reed
Mrs. George W. Reinie
John Renshaw
Henry W. Roden
John N. Rosekrans
David Sachs
Robert P. Seeley
Mrs. J. Francis Shirley
Milton Shoong
Phyllis Silverstein
Mrs. M. C. Sloss
Antonio Sotomayor
Mrs. Jerd Sullivan
Robert M. Taubman
Armstrong Taylor
Derk R. TeRoller
Mrs. Nion R. Tucker
Mr. John R. Upton
Mrs. John R. Upton
William T. Veach
Mrs. Gene Walker
Mrs. John C. Warnecke
Mrs. Fred Watkins
Louis F. Weyand
Brayton Wilbur
Mrs. Donald Wilcox
Harold L. Zellerbach
Stephen A. Zellerbach

San Francisco Civic Ballet Association, 1947 ‡

E. Raymond Armsby
Mrs. Wood Armsby
George Washington Baker
James B. Black
Mrs. Starr Bruce
Allard A. Calkins
George T. Cameron
Frank Clarvoe
Edmond D. Coblentz
Harry D. Collier
Mrs. Sheldon Cooper
William W. Crocker
Tracy Cummings
Mrs. Gardner A. Dailey
Sidney M. Ehrman
Frances A. Elkins
Mrs. Lawrence Fletcher
John F. Forbes
L. M. Giannini
Mrs. Frank R. Girard
Alexander F. Haas
Mrs. Thomas Carr Howe
Edward D. Keil
Mrs. Marcus S. Koshland
Mrs. Lee Laird
Mrs. Roger Lapham Jr.
Dorthy Liebes
Clarence R. Lindner
James K. Lochead
Mrs. John S. Logan
Mrs. Edmunds Lyman
Mrs. Julliard McDonald
Robert Watt Miller
Mrs. Robert Watt Miller
Mrs. Kenneth Monteagle
George Montgomery
D. V. Nicholson
Mrs. Ryer Nixon
Charles Page
Mrs. George Pope Jr.
Mrs. Stanley Powell
John Rosekrans
Mr. William P. Roth
Mrs. William P. Roth
Mrs. M.C. Sloss
Mrs. Jerd F. Sullivan
Mrs. Powers Symington
Mrs. Andrew B. Talbot
Mrs. Richard Tobin
Mrs. Nion R. Tucker
Brayton Wilbur

San Francisco Ballet Association, 1972–2006 *

Mrs. Fernand Abert
Takahide Akiyama
William F. Aldinger
Mrs Frand Aries
David M. Atcheson
Josefina C. Baltodano, JD
Ernest A. Bates, MD
John M. Bates Jr.
Mrs. William Bayless
Hallie A. Beacham, MD
Mrs. Joachim R. Bechtle
Carol L. Benz
John H. Black
Gerald D. Blatherwick
Peter P. Bolles
Mrs. John R. Breeden
Samuel Bronfman II
Sharon Stone Bronstein
Kathleen Brown
Mrs. Harry Camp Jr.
Mrs. G. W. Douglas Carver
Stacey B. Case
Donald E. Casey
Michaela Cassidy
Warren Chinn
Mrs. Gisella Christensen
Harold Christensen
Lew Christensen
Robert Clegg
O. Robert Conkey
Mrs. Charles Crocker
Mrs. Edward Daly
Timothy D. Dattels
Christian de Guigne III
Margot de Wildt
John W. Dewes
Emily Edwards DiLaura
R. Stanley Dollar Jr.
Margot H. Driscoll
Rudolph W. Driscoll
David Duxbury, Esq.
Mrs. Dallas Edgar
Paul A. Eisler, Esq.
Lawrence J. Ellison
Mrs. Douglas J. Engmann
Mrs. Seymour M. Farber
Joseph R. Fink
Robert S. Fisher
T. Jack Foster
Edward Gauer
Richard Gilbert
Judson W. Goldsmith
Steven D. Grand-Jean
Noah Griffin
Adrian Gruhn
Timothy G. Hanlon
Alex Hart
Mrs. Randolph A. Hearst
Mrs. Frederick J. Hellman
John E. Hulse
Patti Hume
John B. Huntington

2005

San Francisco Ballet publicly launches the Performing at the Pinnacle Campaign. It seeks to raise $35 million in new endowment.

San Francisco Ballet wins England's prestigious Laurence Olivier Award, its first, in the category of "Outstanding Achievement in Dance" for its 2004 engagement at London's Sadler's Wells Theatre.

Helgi Tomasson celebrates his twentieth anniversary as artistic director and is awarded the Lew Christensen Medal in recognition of his outstanding contributions to San Francisco Ballet.

San Francisco Ballet performs at the inaugural three-week dance festival Les étés de la danse de Paris. Program includes world premieres by Lar Lubovitch, Paul Taylor, and Christopher Wheeldon.

San Francisco Ballet Association (continued)

Charles E. Johnson
Karla Jurvetson, MD
Edward Karkar
Raymond E. Kassar
John G. Kerns
Ronald L. Kerns
William D. Kimpton
Mrs. Joseph Knowland
Joseph Knowland
Chili Kohlenberg
Elizabeth M. Kramer
Charles S. La Follette
Richard E. LeBlond Jr.
Kimun Lee
Mrs. Irving Levin
Mrs. Davies Lewis
Beth Gerken Logan
John R. Lonergan
W. McNeil Lowry
Charles A. Lynch
Mrs. Donald Magnin
Mr. Leonard Martin
Kenneth Matthews
Mrs. Alexander B. McAllister
John N. McBaine
Mrs. Peter McBean
Norman H. McMillan
Lawrence V. Metcalf
William A. Meyer
Nicola Miner
Stuart G. Moldaw
Michael Moser
Robert A. Muh
Yoh Nakahara
Richard J. Olsen
Mrs. Edgar Osgood
Sherrill A. Parsons
David M. Partridge
Gerd Perkins
Patricia Salas Pineda
Mrs. Michael J. Polenske
Brian M. Powers
John A. Powers
Wayne L. Prim
Mrs. Donald Pritzker
G. Kirk Raab
Barbara L. Rambo
Edward A. Reger Jr.
John H. Reininga Jr.
Mrs. Constance B. Reynolds
Barrett B. Roach
Paul A. MacAulay Robinson
Arthur Rock
Bob Ross
Charles Rueger Jr.
Milton Salkind
Philip S. Schlein
Anne Schmidt
F. Karl Schoenborn
Robert P. Seeley
John E. Sells
Peter N. Sherrill, MD
Walter W. Shervington, MD
Phyllis Silverstein
Allen J. Simon
Ronald R. Sloan

Michael Smuin
Robert A. Swanson
Mrs. Melvin M. Swig
Richard L. Swig
Joyce Taylor
Susan Tohbe
Senator Art Torres (ret.)
Darrow Tully
Sidney Unobskey
Mrs. John R. Upton
Ann Wagner
Mrs. John C. Warnecke
Phyllis C. Wattis
Carolyn Wean
Karen Wegmann
Keith West, MD
Harry W. Wilcott
Mrs. Donald Wilcox
E.B. Wilson
Sharon Y. Woo
Harold L. Zellerbach
Jan Zones

+ In 1933, Gaetano Merola, founding director of San Francisco Opera, established the San Francisco Opera Ballet. Until 1942, the Opera Ballet and its School remained under the jurisdiction of the San Francisco Opera. Therefore, this list includes the San Francisco Opera Association Board Leadership, 1933–1941. Furthermore, programs between 1933 and 1937 indicate that the San Francisco Opera Ballet was presented under the auspices of the San Francisco Opera Women's Committtee. Consequently, these members are also included here. Please note that a list of the San Francisco Opera Women's Committtee in 1934 could not be located at the Performing Arts Library and Museum, where archives for San Francisco Ballet are stored.

† Willam and Harold Christensen renamed the company San Francisco Ballet after purchasing it from the San Francisco Opera in 1942. Between 1942 and 1971, the Ballet's governing body was known as the San Francisco Ballet Guild. Please note that lists for the San Francisco Ballet Guild for 1946, 1948, 1949, 1950, 1951, 1957, and 1958 could not be located at the Performing Arts Library and Museum, where archives for San Francisco Ballet are stored.

‡ In 1947, the San Francisco Civic Ballet Association was created as a body of civic leaders dedicated to raising funds for the Ballet. The Association existed in addition to the San Francisco Ballet Guild. The San Francisco Ballet Civic Ballet Association lasted for only one year.

* Since 1972, the Ballet's governing body has been known as the San Francisco Ballet Association. This list is as of November 1, 2006.

San Francisco Ballet Orchestra

Music Director and Principal Conductor

Martin West

Violin I

Roy Malan, Concertmaster
Janice McIntosh,
    Associate Concertmaster
Beni Shinohara, Assistant Concertmaster
Heidi Wilcox
Mia Kim
Robin Hansen
Brian Lee
Mariya Borozina

Violin II

Marianne Wagner, Principal
Craig Reiss, Associate Principal
Yehudit Lieberman, Assistant Principal
Patricia Van Winkle
Clifton Foster
Elbert Tsai *
Adrienne Duckworth **

Viola

Paul Ehrlich, Principal
Anna Kruger, Associate Principal
Leonore Kish, Assistant Principal
Susan Bates
Caroline Lee

Cello

David Kadarauch, Principal
Eric Sung, Associate Principal
Victor Fierro, Assistant Principal
Thalia Moore
Nora Pirquet

Contrabass

Steve D'Amico, Principal
Shinji Eshima, Associate Principal
Jonathan Lancelle, Assistant Principal
Mark Drury

Flute

Barbara Chaffe, Principal *
Julie McKenzie, Acting Principal
Patricia Farrell, 2nd & Piccolo **

Oboe

Liang Wang, Principal *
Laura Griffiths, Acting Principal **
Marilyn Coyne, 2nd & English Horn

Clarinet

Carey Bell, Acting Principal **
James Dukey, 2nd & Bass Clarinet

Bassoon

Rufus Olivier, Principal
David Bartolotta, 2nd & Contrabassoon

Horn

Elizabeth Freimuth, Principal *
Bill Klingelhoffer, Acting Principal
Keith Green
Brian McCarty, Associate Principal
Lawrence Ragent **

Trumpet/Cornet

Charles Metzger, Principal
Ralph Wagner

Trombone

Jeffrey Budin, Principal
Hall Goff

Bass Trombone

Scott Thornton, Principal

Tuba

Peter Wahrhaftig, Principal

Timpani

James Gott, Principal

Percussion

David Rosenthal, Principal

Harp

Marcella DeCray, Principal

Personnel Manager

Tom Rose

Music Librarian

Matthew Naughtin

* On Leave of Absence
** Season Substitute

2006

San Francisco Ballet performs for the first time as part of New York's Lincoln Center Festival.

San Francisco Ballet is the first non-European company named "Company of the Year" in *Dance Europe* magazine's annual readers' poll.

2007

San Francisco Ballet performs in Reykjavik, Iceland.

San Francisco Ballet Orchestra, led by Martin West, music director and principal conductor, produces new recording of *Nutcracker*.

2008

San Francisco Ballet celebrates its 75th anniversary with a two-week festival of world premiere works by ten choreographers.

San Francisco Ballet Staff

HELGI TOMASSON
Artistic Director & Choreographer

GLENN McCOY
Executive Director

Lesley Koenig
General Manager

Thomas W. Flynn
Director of Development

Julie A. Begley
Director of Marketing & Communications

Martin West
Music Conductor and Principal Conductor

Lola de Avila
Associate Director—SF Ballet School

Kim Ondreck Carim
Chief Financial Officer

Charles Chip McNeal
Director of Education

Steven Kaster
Director of Information Services

Artistic

Ashley Wheater
*Ballet Master & Assistant
to the Artistic Director*

Betsy Erickson, Anita Paciotti
Ballet Mistresses

Ricardo Bustamante
Ballet Master

Yuri Possokhov
Choreographer in Residence

Regina Bustillos
Personal Assistant to Mr. Tomasson

Alan Takata-Villareal
Scheduling Administrator

Rose Gutierrez
Assistant to the Artistic Staff

Production

Lefty Lefcourt
Assistant Techinal Director

Kevin Connaughton
Lighting Supervisor

Jane Green
Stage Manager

Tiffani Snow
Assistant Stage Manager

Nixon Bracisco
Master Carpenter

Dennis Hudson
Master Electrician

Kenneth M. Ryan
Master of Properties

Kevin Kirby
Audio Engineer

Kevin Rogers
Flyman

George Elvin
Wardrobe Supervisor

Patti Fitzpatrick
Costume Supervisor

Richard Battle
Make-Up and Wig Supervisor

Robin Church
Wig and Hair Stylist

Sherri LeBlanc
Company Shoe Administrator

Company Management

Robert Russo
Company Manager

Jane Shaffer
Operations Coordinator

Evan Wagoner-Lynch
Operations Assistant

Music

Michael McGraw, Nina Pinzarrone,
Natal'ya Feygina
Company Pianists

Roy Malan
Concertmaster

Tom Rose
Orchestra Personnel Manager

Matthew Naughtin
Music Librarian

Administration

Cecelia Beam
Human Resources Manager

Jennifer French Kovacevich
*Board Relations Manager &
75th Anniversary Project Coordinator*

Valerie M. Byrnes
*Administrative Assistant to the
Executive Director*

Development

Winifred Appleby
Associate Director of Development

Stephanie Ziesel
Associate Director of Development

Allison K. Groves
Planned Giving Manager

Don Brown
*Manager of Corporate and
Foundation Relations*

Sarah Rhyins
*Manager of Christensen Society
and Membership*

Cate Czerwinski
Research and Stewardship Manager

Fermin Nasol
Major Gifts Officer

Jayson Johnson
Christensen Society Officer

Amanda Frederickson
Special Events Assistant

Kristi DeCaminada
Assistant to the Director of Development

Jill Lounibos
Grants Associate

Ruben Fonseca
Sponsorship and Corporate Giving Associate

Kati Robbins
Membership Associate

Nicole Frydman
Development Associate

Maya Lawrence
Individual Gifts Assistant

Lynn Noonan
Principal Gifts Consultant

Marketing & Communications

Daryl Carr
*Associate Director of
Marketing & Communications*

Betsy Lindsey
*Associate Director,
Ticket and Patron Services*

Kyra Jablonsky
Associate Director, Public Relations

Beth Hondl
Senior Marketing and Sales Manager

Valerie Megas
Merchandise Manager

Sarah Reiwitch
Webmaster

Alison Aves
Editorial Manager

Meredith Nonnenberg
Public Relations Associate

Carmen Rickenbach
Graphics Coordinator

Erik Almlie
Image Archivist

Victoria Andújar
Public Relations Assistant

Ticket Services

Jennifer Peterian
Box Office Manager/Treasurer

Jennifer Hughes
1st Assistant Treasurer

Sharon Handa
Assistant Treasurer

David Clark
Phone Room Supervisor

Edith Bryson, McKenzie Charles,
Mary Colby, Jennifer Cooley,
Trudy Dorrell, Evan James, Oktay Kozak,
Katrina Magee, Gene Morrison,
Patricia Pearson, Courtney Pheils,
Dax Proctor, Cherryl Usi
Ticket Sales Associates

Finance

Emma Huckabay
Controller

Ann Truong
Senior Accountant

Minda Salinas
Payroll Coordinator

Kim Nguyen-Ly
Staff Accountant

Maritza Choriego
Accounting Assistant

Facilities

Jason Blackwell
Facilities Manager

Andrew Harvill
Facilities Supervisor

Royce Waldon
Facilities Coordinator

Michael DeGroot, Todd Martin,
Donald Newt
Facilities Assistants

Tamara de la Cruz, Katharine Winn
Receptionist

Information Services

Gary Escobedo
Help Desk & Systems Administrator

Karen Irvin
Database Administrator & Reports Specialist

Steven Zawadzski
Database Programmer

SF Ballet School

Helgi Tomasson
Director

Faculty

Lola de Avila, Shannon Bresnahan,
Yoira Esquivel Brito, Kristi DeCaminada,
Jorge Esquivel, Pascale Leroy,
Jeffrey Lyons, Parrish Maynard

Anna Baker
Music

Leonid Shagalov
Character

Leslie Young
Trainee Program Coordinator

Charles Chip McNeal
Dance in Schools

Pianists

Alla Gladysheva, Maya Gorodetsky,
Lynn Inglese, Anna Karney,
Jamie Narushchen, Eleonora Shevkhod,
Laura Tishchenko, Larisa Tsodikov,
Galina Umanskaya

School Administration

Jim Sohm
Administrative Manager

Kirsten Gamb
Registrar

Brianna Dwyer-O'Connor
Administrative Assistant

Pete Ippel
Residence Manager

Patricia Swanson
Residence Assistant

Center for Dance Education

Dina D. Toy
Education Office Manager

Stacey Blakeman
*Dance in Schools and Communities
Coordinator*

Cecelia Beam
Adult Education Coordinator

Dance in Schools &
Community Staff

Kimberly Agnew, Daniel Berkman,
James Brosnahan III, Daniel Frazier,
Lynn Inglese, Erica Rose Jeffrey,
Melanie Mitchell, Zeke Nealy,
Wade Peterson, Emily Pitcher,
Jeni Swerdlow, Will Waghorn,
Kirsten Williams

Company Physicians

Richard Gibbs, M.D.
Medical Supervisor

John Callander, M.D., Peter Callandar,
M.D., Keith Donatto
Supervising Orthopedists

Leonard Stein, D.C.
Chiropractic Care

Frederic Bost, M.D., Jon Dickinson,
M.D., Robert Ganburd, M.D.
Orthopedic Advisors to the Company

Michael Leslie
Company Physical Therapist

Karl Schmetz
Consulting Physical Therapist

Floriana Alessandria
Medical Administrator

Photo Credits

© Howard Amidon: 99

© Steven Caras: 85

© Lloyd Englert: 8–9, 24, 30, 92, 127, 143, 148

© Andrea Flores: 68, 109, 137

© Thomas John Gibbons: 153

© Mark Hanauer: 19

© Chris Hardy: 4–7, 14–15, 16–17, 114, 118, 119 (right), 144–145

© Dan Krauss: 94

© George Kruse: 36

© Terrence McCarthy: 22

© Jacques Moatti: 58, 76–77

© Ray "Scotty" Morris: 55

© Marty Sohl: 33, 65, 78–79, 115, 161

© Martha Swope: 80, 85, 91

© Erik Tomasson: cover, 2–3, 10–13, 20–21, 28, 31, 34–35, 39, 42–53, 56–57, 60–61, 64, 67, 69–73, 75, 86–87, 89, 93, 95, 96–98, 101, 102–104, 108–109, 110–113, 119 (left), 120–126, 129–132, 136, 140–142, 146–147, 149–152, 154, 158–159, 162–165

© Weiferd Watts: 128

Index

Pages in italics indicate photos.

31901046183655